JUMP!

Now You Will Have No Excuse

By Scott "Spiderman" Mulholland

First Printing 2017

ISBN: 978-0-692-78881-3

US Building Consultants, Inc.
1722 NW 80th Blvd., Ste. 70
Gainesville, FL 32606

www.spidermans.com

I dedicate this book to my Lord Jesus Christ who took me from a broken childhood, a garbage can and an otherwise hopeless state, into a successful husband, father and entrepreneur who has lived the life of three people. I am thankful for His many mercies and kindnesses in my life. He not only delivered me from my own self-destructive nature, He allowed me to have a great family and friends who have made huge impacts on my success.

I would also like to dedicate this book to my beloved wife and children. They have given me the inspiration and passion to drive me far beyond most men with similarly limited abilities and handicaps from past trauma. No expression or words could ever convey how they have supported and loved me despite my short comings. My wife, especially, has been so loving and kind to me and has been a tremendous support over our 35 years of marriage. I will be forever grateful for finding a treasure like her to spend my life and raise a family with.

Table of Chapters

Preface

Introduction

Chapter 1: The Day the Visits Ended   1

Chapter 2: Losing Another Mother   9

Chapter 3: The Loneliness of Life   13

Chapter 4: Becoming Numb to Life   17

Chapter 5: Losing My Hero   21

Chapter 6: Losing My Purpose in Life   25

Chapter 7: Losing My Dad   29

Chapter 8: Life as a Foster Kid   35

Chapter 9: Learning to Run Away   39

Chapter 10: Being Abused Becomes a Part of Life   45

Chapter 11: Seeing Dad Again   51

Chapter 12: In the System Again   59

Chapter 13: Alcohol Finally Destroys My Relationship with Mom 64

Chapter 14: Being Sent Away   71

Chapter 15: Living on the Streets   77

Chapter 16: Kidnapped in China Town   81

Chapter 17: The Streets Took a Toll on Me   86

Chapter 18: Meeting Joe   126

Chapter 19: Someone Was Looking for a Few Good Men   137

Chapter 20: Culture Shock, Becoming a Marine   143

Chapter 21: Becoming a U.S. Marine Corps Sniper   150

Chapter 22: Training in Special Operations   157

Chapter 23: The Accident That Changed My Life   165

Chapter 24: The Book Was Right, Not the Preacher   175

Chapter 25: Finding My Soul Mate   180

Chapter 26: Giving Up My Life's Career Ambition   186

Chapter 27: Becoming an Entrepreneur   197

Chapter 28: "Spiderman" Gets His Name   202

Chapter 29: Learning About Business the Hard Way   205

Chapter 30: Losing It All Should Not Stop You   210

Chapter 31: I Could Have Made Excuses, but I Became Successful
Instead   215

Chapter 32: The Best Part of My Story   220

Chapter 33: Finding and Forgiving My Mother   227

Chapter 34: What Excuses Are Holding You Back?   234

Chapter 35: Good Luck to You All   241

This book contains the true story of how I went from living in a dumpster on Seattle's skid row to becoming the Corporate CEO of three multi-million dollar companies.

The above photo was shot as I was revisiting downtown Seattle, Christmas holidays, 2011. In the background, is the 43 story Ivers Smith Tower that I scaled and worked on as a beginner window cleaner back on the streets in 1977.

You simply cannot kill someone

who refuses to die…

Preface

Many times throughout my life, I have heard people come up with a laundry list of reasons, actually just lame excuses, for why they haven't achieved their goals. To label them as excuses may sound a bit harsh and unsympathetic to some people, but the world can be a very harsh and unsympathetic place. That, my friends, is the first thing you must realize to move forward.

Some say the reason for their failure is because, "My Dad never said, 'I love you' to me," or "I grew up in the ghetto without any money." Others say, "My parents were control freaks, and it drove me off the deep end." Still, others defend their poor performance by saying such things as "My parents were on drugs, they were alcoholics, and they abused me, beat me, molested me, or took advantage of me." Some tell me they just never seemed to get a single break in life, or even that they feel that life has cursed them.

Welcome to the defeatist camp, friends; it's a huge one, full of millions of sadly misinformed people who feel like failures.

The truth is, no matter what has happened to you, or whatever adversity you currently face, you have not been personally singled out for mistreatment and failure. And you are not alone in feeling mistreated. If you sense you are, you are working under a perception handicap because of the baggage you are carrying from your past, self-destructive baggage you are pointlessly lugging behind you from your upbringing or from the disappointing way life has unfolded for you.

However, you don't have to stay handicapped! You don't have to stay stuck in this swamp of self-pity, bitterly blaming others for your misfortunes and failure to reach your goals. If you are ever to get ahead, as a matter of fact, you must relinquish these falsehoods and accept the truth that if you would be authentically successful, it's all up to you. Only you can change your situation and only after you stop whining, blaming, and making excuses. Armed with this incorrigible fact of life, you are then capable of accomplishing anything!

I was inspired to write this book to tear at the very fabric of the destructive lies put into the minds of many confused, floundering, and suffering people by their therapists, doctors, and counselors who try to help them. For I get angry whenever I hear about another small child forced onto medication or into counseling or therapy that indirectly brainwashes the child into thinking he or she will be successful if only he or she accepts their version of the world, agrees with their psychological diagnoses and swallows their prescribed medications. Nothing could be less helpful to such people.

Through my own difficult origins and subsequent life experiences and studies, I have come to firmly believe that you can become anything you choose to be in your life, however poor your circumstances were growing up in this world and whatever obstacles you face today and must overcome.

Again, it's up to you. You can do it. However, personal change comes only from within.

Nevertheless, change is also learned. If you don't want to be a loser or feel like a failure anymore, you have to learn to change your mindset and behavior to become a winner. You must develop the attitude, frame of mind, and methodologies of a winner. If you convince a person that he is a loser, he will likely always be one. Barring a fundamental change in his perception of himself and his philosophy of life, he will probably never become anything more than a loser. It's pretty much a law of human nature.

We all aspire only to whom and what we think we are fundamental in life. To address this problem on a large scale, I think we need a paradigm shift in how we train, school, influence, encourage, and develop people to become exceptional, creative beings who lead moral, stable, and productive lives in our society. However, you, as an individual, can autonomously create within yourself a paradigm shift that will lay the groundwork for a new and more productive, positive you. Yes, a successful you!

"How?", you ask. By reading the account within the pages of this book of how I overcame severe disadvantages, re-framed my self-concept, and found my faith. Moreover, perhaps most of all, by persisting.

That is my real purpose in writing this book. I want to clearly lay out the techniques that have proven so successful for me in overcoming a horrible childhood, having faced many of the issues I mentioned earlier, to become a successful entrepreneur, building multi-million dollar businesses and happily on my way to building more.

We all have the power and creative ability given to us by God to be anyone or anything we want to be in life. When you honestly think, feel, or say that you will never be successful in life or an asset to society, you're probably right.

However, when you honestly think, feel, and say that you can and will be successful in life, no matter what, you will lead an extraordinary life.

But do not misunderstand. Many ambitious people equate success with the acquisition of large sums of money and ignore the human quotient and relationship dimension of life. They spend all their time amassing large sums of money, but once their bank balance and asset portfolio are pumped up sky-high, they find themselves terribly lonely and socially isolated. Perhaps they've stepped on people, steamrolled or exploited people to get to the top. This often happens.

Then suddenly one day they realize they are absolutely miserable and the only people in their world who "make nice" to them are after their money. Their "friends" are nothing more than groupies and hangers-on who are always on the make and always have their hands out for a handout.

Readers, this type of selfish individual has made some serious mistakes in judgment, maybe so serious, depending on how many people he's alienated and how badly his reputation has been damaged, as to be irremediable. Such a person may have doomed himself to remain alone, forever shunned by decent society, regardless of his great wealth, as an undesirable. Sadly, he wakes up one day and suddenly sees clearly that the only people who want to be around him are gold diggers and parasites, certainly no one who truly cares for him or feels any real love for him.

Such a one has totally missed the point. Moreover, the point is that life without the sincere love and staunch support of friends and family who really care is a life not worth living.

In spite of my many business successes and professional accomplishments, if I were to lose the love of my beloved wife Tina and my treasured children and grandchildren, if my dear and loyal friends would for some reason fall away or become estranged from me, my life would be airless, joyless and meaningless. I might as well be dead. All my strivings would have amounted to nothing.

One must never lose sight of this signal truth. Never. For if you do, even for a nanosecond, you risk alienating and losing the most valuable assets anyone could have on earth. Your most priceless possessions are your times alone with God, family and friends. You will find, as everyone eventually does, that nothing is more important than your faith in God and the company of good people who really care for you, people who will stand by you and encourage you, no matter what happens, through thick and thin, and without reference to how much money you have.

No, real peace and satisfaction are only found in being faithful to God and in loving, caring relationships built on honesty and trust. The challenge for all of us in life is to become what it is that we honestly want to be, no matter the odds against us, and whatever it takes.

This book is the true story of how I overcame incredible odds as a young boy to become a successful businessman, a loving husband, and father to four terrific children and grandfather to three outstanding grandchildren, and a unique self-confident individual. It is about how I created a stable, balanced, and well-rounded life for myself and family. It is about my profound inner transformation into someone whom I feel is a productive, active asset to today's society, a genuinely "good person," and a responsible citizen.

I pray this story will inspire and convince you that nothing is impossible for those who dare to believe and who put forth the honest effort to try their utmost to achieve their goals. I hope this book will remove all illusions about what it takes to get ahead and that reading it leaves you with no excuses or alibis for why you cannot succeed. You can succeed, and you better believe it.

Get ready to be challenged like you have never been before.

Scott "Spiderman" Mulholland

Introduction

Yes, my name really is "Spiderman."

Yes, I really do climb up and rappel down the sides of high-rise buildings and swing on ropes across the face of them from forty and fifty stories above the ground.

Yes, I am probably a bit crazy - but in a very good way, I'd like to think.

No, taking on the name "Spiderman" and doing all these high flying dangerous things in my work is not a gimmick. In aggregate, it is a way of life that I pursue because I love it. I have a passion for it and my other motivations will become clear to you as you read through the pages of this book.

"Spiderman." It's not just a nickname or what people call me. "Spiderman" is, in fact, part of my legal name and I currently have a confidential agreement on the legal trademark with the name and Marvel Comics.

However, it is much more than just my real name, because "Spiderman" is who I am inside. He is that part of me I have become, a living actualization or embodiment of the strength I had to acquire to deal with the challenges, fear, and dangers I had to face and overcome just to survive growing up. You don't swing from rope fifty stories up the side of a high-rise building if you are not completely focused, very sure of your skills and completely confident in yourself, your equipment, and your abilities. That all comes from within, and it took me a long time to develop the mindset to take on everything else in life—confidently, fearlessly—in the same way I do when flying across the sides of buildings.

That's who and what "Spiderman" Mulholland is. I am he, knowing myself, completely self-aware, comfortable with my past and who I really am today. I am Spiderman, having discovered my true inner identity and running with it. I am most fully myself in finding strength in the archetypal superhero character Spiderman with whom I can identify, personify and use to help myself be successful every day, in everything I try to do in my life, in spite of the odds I have to face and the obstacles I have to overcome.

Equipped with this self-knowledge and the Spiderman avatar of cunning and invincibility, I didn't make excuses; I didn't give up on becoming somebody just because of the bad things that had happened to me growing up. I survived those events and then thrived from the knowledge and valuable lessons learned from them. Ultimately, they made me stronger after having experienced and survived them because I learned invaluable lessons I could not have learned otherwise. Lessons absorbed at the deepest level, which then made me stronger and shaped and molded me into the person I am today.

You can too.

This book is a peeling away at the layers of my life that have helped me become a successful business person. The first part is not fun and may be a bit uncomfortable for some to read, but it was my reality. I have not minced words or softened any of the events or violent incidents. They are included here in perhaps hair-raising detail for the sake of honesty to make my point. That point is how I overcame a horrible and terrifying childhood to become a strong, confident, and successful person and a businessman.

The process of writing this book has been surprisingly therapeutic for me. I was able to re-live troubling, painful experiences, reflect upon their ultimate meaning in my life and achieve closure and peace upon realizing the vital roles they played in making me the person I am today.

The result, I hope, will give readers what I have found to be a collection of useful tools, maybe even a whole toolbox worth of tools, that will enable readers to construct the mindset necessary to becoming successful in life and in business, whatever odds you may face.

The Day the Visits Ended

"There ain't no way you can hold onto something that wants to go, you understand? You can only love what you got while you got it."

—Kate DiCamillo, Because of Winn-Dixie

Chapter 1
The Day the Visits Ended

It was visitation time again.

I was only four years old, but I still remember that last regularly scheduled visit I had with my Mom as if it were yesterday. My Mom and Dad had been separated for about a year at the time, and I had weekends with Mom on a regular basis. My brothers Tim, Brett, Jay, Gerald, and I lived with my Dad in a big blue two-story house in Forcevilla, Washington, while my little sister Lisa lived with my Mom.

My Mom had me all weekend, and up to this point, it had been a great visit. Now it was over, and I sat next to Mom in the front seat as she drove down the interstate to take me back to my Dad's house. That was when she gave me the news that we couldn't visit each other anymore.

After she had told me, as soon as the words had sunk in, I felt a wave of fear and shock race through my body. I couldn't speak. My lips would not move. I couldn't answer her. She started crying.

"You don't love me anymore?", I finally managed to mumble. "Is that why I don't live with you anymore?" I felt fear and rejection.

"No, honey," she replied softly, lovingly, "I love you more than anything in this world, but right now, we just can't."

"The reason we can't see each other anymore," she told me that day, "is because a judge has ruled me to be unfit to take care of you."

Sometime later, I found out she had been deemed a threat to her children because she supposedly had tried to kill us. I didn't remember her ever trying to kill us. But when she drank, she hit us and got angry with

Dad, and they would end up getting in brutal fights. When that happened, she didn't seem like herself.

I remembered the old, cozy family room in our house; a sliding door separated it from the kitchen. Despite the closed door, the yelling and sounds of fighting still poured through. Unfortunately, my parents fought a lot and even more unfortunately, drinking fueled those arguments. Whenever it happened, I shook and cried as fear filled my mind. When I looked at my brothers, they seemed to be just as scared as I was.

I should say all of this didn't just happen overnight. Mom's mean, erratic behavior toward us had started early and, with very few exceptions, had been consistent all our lives.

From the time I was just two-years-old, Mom had kicked me out of the house routinely, and I had sought refuge at a wonderfully kind neighbor's house. Her name was and is Kathy Hoppenrath. She had a family of her own, but she took me in, fed me, and gave me a place to sleep. She even did my laundry. She and my Dad had sort of come to an agreement that she would take care of both me and my younger brother Gerald. My older brother Tim looked out for my other brothers while Dad was at work. Kathy's generosity is very likely the reason I survived my Mom's unpredictable violence. Kathy's family became a like a loving family to me. Over time, I grew to think of Kathy's home as my home, and I even called her "Mom." The Hoppenraths were all very encouraging and caring. I don't think I could have made it without them.

Even so, I still genuinely loved my Mom. She really was a good mother to us, always taking good care of me, and playing with me. When she held me, I felt safe, and my fear disappeared. Nevertheless, the fighting always took all the fun out of her and my Dad.

Sometimes the yelling was so loud that I shut my eyes and covered my ears to block it out. In bed at night, my body trembled, and I continued to shake until I awoke in the morning. Many times, I was awakened during the evening by the sound of Mom and Dad's fighting. I hid under the covers, curled up in a ball, crying. I felt so scared all the time. It was always quiet for a long time after the fighting ended.

At the time, I didn't understand the reason for my parents' separation, as well as the court's sudden, incomprehensible decision to terminate visitation. When Mom was hurt and angry, she drank and ended up hurting us, sometimes very badly. But my Mom never hurt me except when she drank, so I always forgave her when, the next day, she acted normal and as if she really cared for us. But she kept drinking, probably to offset her volatile relationship with my Dad. One night she kicked me hard in the stomach, and I ended up going to the hospital. Because of her attack on me, my Dad hit her, and then she hit him back. That was when he knocked her to the floor. I remember her lying there hurt, but she just kept yelling at him.

As my Dad took me to the hospital, he promised me that it would never happen again. That was when the court-ordered split and visitations began.

As she dropped me off at home that day for the last time, I couldn't feel my arms or legs. They felt numb all over, and the knot in my stomach hurt terribly.

"Why? Why? Why?" I kept asking her, but her answers just couldn't seem to make the questions stop coming.

"Why can't we see each other?" I cried.

It just didn't make any sense to me. I didn't understand why this was happening to me. I loved my Mom so much, and I hated having to wait until the weekends to see her. I missed her so badly, and it always seemed like it took so long for Saturdays to come.

As we walked back into the house that day, Mom and Dad fought again. This one was a bad fight and Mom cried a lot. Then, it just stopped.

Mom came over and hugged me for a long time. I always felt so safe when I was in her arms. She wasn't like our babysitter, who was always horrible to me and confined me to my room all day long.

My Mom's touch always calmed me and my body always stopped shaking when she held me. Now, as she held me, all my fears went away, and for a few seconds, it seemed as if things could just get better. I guess I was letting myself hope it was somehow only a big mistake and that suddenly everything would be back to normal.

Then she began to cry, hard this time. She hugged each of my brothers and me one by one, then turned and walked down the steps to the door.

This time, she didn't say, "I'll see you next week."

My body shook, and my older brother Brett grabbed me so I couldn't run after her. Mom never turned around so I could see her face. Suddenly I couldn't breathe. No matter how hard I tried, I couldn't seem to get enough air. I hyperventilated as I ran to a bedroom to get a last glimpse of her leaving. I jumped up on the bed and watched out the big window overlooking the driveway.

I could see her walking to her car. I screamed and banged frantically on the window. She stopped, turned around, and looked up to the window at me. I screamed at her to come back. She stood there silently, frozen in place. I saw silent tears running down her face.

She smiled at me, but it wasn't her real smile, then she blew me a brave kiss. That's when she finally couldn't hold it back anymore. Sobbing, she quickly turned her head away so I wouldn't see her crying. I lost it and started banging on the window again. Dad was on my right shoulder and Brett was to my left, trying to pull me away, but I just kept clawing at the window. I remember thinking that if I could only go through it, I could get to my Mom.

By now, I was breathing hard, and my body was jerking and shaking with fear at the possibility of never seeing my mother again. I don't remember ever jerking out of fear before that awful day, but the thought of never seeing her again filled me with a feeling of complete terror. I began to feel dizzy and my stomach started hurting badly.

I kept screaming and banging on the window, but my Mom wouldn't look up again. She quickly pulled out of the driveway and was gone. My Dad and Brett forced me onto the bed and everything went black.

Someone held a paper bag over my mouth, and I could hear my Dad saying, "Breathe! Breathe!" However, I couldn't.

I don't remember much of what happened next on that day. In fact, many things that happened after my Mom left that day have disappeared; only bits and pieces occasionally come to me.

A long, long time went by before I would see her again. In fact, I can't remember her even calling us on the phone to talk. In her wisdom, I'm sure she realized it was much easier on everyone that way, especially the kids.

During those days, I climbed into my Dad's lap and hugged him as hard as I could. He hugged me back or rubbed his whiskers on my face, which always hurt but still made me laugh. The funny thing was, even though he was big and strong and was my Dad, when he hugged me, I still felt scared. His hugs weren't like my Mom's; somehow, her hugs made everything all right. They made me feel safe.

I needed that; I was always scared in that house at night without Mom there. I guess a big part of the reason I was so scared, was because of some rather frightening woodcarvings that hung in the house, with scary faces in them.

In my childhood imagination, they seemed to come alive at night and lurk out there, just waiting for a chance to get me. I hated going to bed; I always imagined that any minute now, they would come to attack me.

I tried to sleep with Dad, but he wouldn't let me, so I stayed under my covers, trembling and shaking throughout the night until the morning light awakened me.

Whenever I woke up during the night, I always hoped it would be morning already. If not, I pretended to sleep so the creatures from the woodcarvings would not hurt me; as long as they thought I was sleeping, they couldn't get me. I hated being the only one awake at night when my brothers were sleeping; I always felt so alone.

Sometimes, when I thought that the Indians — the wooden faces in the carvings — were coming after me, I screamed as loud as I could, and Dad ran down the stairs. My screaming would always scare my brothers and then they cried too. When we talked about it many years later, Brett and Jay admitted that they were also scared at night and imagined men dressed as Indians and the wooden faces on the wall coming to life to get them.

I also remember hating it when Dad went to work and didn't take me. At that point in time, my Dad delivered milk to people's doorsteps for Smith Dairy Farms and sometimes he took me along on his delivery route since I did not like staying home with the babysitter. She was not at all like my Mom, and I told her so, many times. Maybe that's why she never liked me, but I didn't care about that at all, I was just angry with her for trying to be like my Mom.

Losing Another Mother

"Some people come into our lives and quickly go.
Some stay for a while, leave footprints on our
hearts, and we are never, ever the same."

—Flavia Weedn, <u>Forever</u>

Chapter 2
Losing Another Mother

Years passed, and I kept living with the fear at night and missing my Mom, but then my Dad met a woman named Sally and I wound up getting used to someone else. Sally was a good person and very attractive. She had two boys named Randy and Robby; it was always great to play with them.

Sally made me feel like Mom did when she held me, but she held everyone, especially Randy. I could get Sally to hug me, and it stopped the shaking, but she just didn't have the same touch that my Mom had.

One day some time later, my Dad announced that he was going to marry Sally. When I heard him say it, I suddenly grew so angry inside that I started shaking all over. I asked him if he was just going to forget about our real Mom now and he promptly sent me to my room.

It wasn't too long afterward that Dad and Sally did get married. While always nice to me, she kept her distance. She wasn't strong like my Mom, and she seemed to get upset easily. Unlike my Mom, she always told my Dad when I did something wrong, and he beat me with the belt. He hit my arms, legs, and back hard. When he came home angry or in a bad mood, he sometimes whipped me and wouldn't stop. I tried to crawl up the wall to get away from the sting of the belt.

My life went on like this for a while, with me feeling mostly normal but I was always missing Mom and having moments of sheer terror and pain. Then one day, Dad made another announcement and told us we were going to have a little sister.

This time, I was happy about it since my real sister Lisa lived with my mother and I hadn't seen her since Mom left. I was excited about Sally having a baby girl and us having another baby sister.

At this time, my Dad sold real estate and made lots of money. We moved into a big house on a lake, where we had a cool boat. We seemed to be doing well, and I wasn't as scared being in the new house. I slept with my younger brother Gerald, who didn't seem scared at all, which helped me a great deal.

Soon, our new little sister Kathy was born, adding to our already big family — now seven boys and two girls, counting Lisa and Sally's boys. Things seemed to turn around for our family during this time. I could sleep okay at night now and hardly ever woke up shaking anymore. I remember the feeling of happiness and sometimes, even joy becoming a part of my life.

It was wonderful.

Then, when I was about ten, my Dad suffered a nervous breakdown and was hit hard with depression afterward. I wouldn't find out the reason until almost twenty-five years later. The IRS had gone after him for back taxes from real estate deals that he didn't think were taxable because of a partnership in which he was involved.

In the end, he was assessed penalty after penalty, along with the massive interest that had accumulated over the three or four years it had been past due. This didn't affect me much. At my age, I didn't understand it at all, and I was never told back then exactly what was wrong.

It wasn't long before we lost our big, beautiful house on the lake, along of course with the boat and our cars. Things became rough

11

financially, but at first, that just seemed to draw us closer together as a family. Eventually, however, the financial pressure was too much for Sally, and after only a few years of marriage, she left us without notice, taking Randy, Robby, and Kathy with her. I watched my Dad suffer through another nervous breakdown, on top of what he was already experiencing.

Sure enough, my nightmares returned, as my life once again became unstable and shaken.

Everything seemed to be in constant turmoil, and I cried a lot. Despite everything, though, he did what he could. People cooked dinner for us and slept over at our little apartment. Sometimes ladies I didn't know showed up and tried to help, but they never stayed long.

A situation that included a very depressed and shattered man, along with five confused and despondent boys, didn't create a very enticing or healthy environment for a relationship at any level.

The Loneliness of Life

"See, I think there are roads that lead us to each other. But in my family, there were no roads - just underground tunnels. I think we all got lost in those underground tunnels. No, not lost. We just lived there."

—Benjamin Alire Sáenz, Last Night I Sang to the Monster

Chapter 3
The Loneliness of Life

Babysitters became a way of life for us again, as Dad struggled to make a living as a used car salesperson, with very low self-esteem. Over the next year or so, while Dad went to work, he left my brothers and me at home alone. He worked twelve- to sixteen-hour days at the car lot, sometimes seven days a week, trying to support us boys and pay child support for Lisa.

Times being what they were, it wasn't long before drugs, alcohol, and cigarettes became a way of life for Brett and Jay, and therefore for me too.

Whenever they ran out of cigarettes, they sent me to the store to steal more for them. Because I was so small and innocent looking, I had become a professional shoplifter by the time I was eleven years old. Therefore, I drank, smoked, took drugs, and stole at the ripe old age of eleven, mostly just for the attention.

As insurance, sometimes I stole a few extra cartons of cigarettes and hid them in the house. Whenever I got lonely, I pulled out a carton and instantly, for a short time, my brothers, their friends, and girlfriends loved me. I would be the center of attention. It never lasted, though; as soon as the carton was gone, so was the attention.

By the time I was twelve years old, I was hooked on cigarettes, sometimes smoking half a pack a day. I even smoked my Dad's pipe and stripped his cigarette butts, just to ease the addiction in my small body. During this time, I didn't seem to shake or have nightmares anymore, but when things got bad, I smoked, drank, or took whatever medication I could find in my Dad's medicine cabinet.

At other times, my brothers gave me pot to smoke, and then they all sat back and laughed while I choked and got so high that I freaked out and suffered panic attacks. I enjoyed the attention I got from them when this happened, which made me do it more and more. Regardless of the thrill, or the attention, I still missed my sisters and my Mom during this time. It didn't wipe away that loss.

Kathy was three years old the last time I saw her. After thirty-six years, I never saw her or found out how she was doing. Sally broke off all contact with us when she left us. I carried around the guilt for that all my life; my Dad very clearly told my brothers and me that we were the reason Sally left . . . especially me. He said we were just too much for her to handle.

School did not go well for me during this time either. Since the age of eight or nine, doctors put me in a special education class and prescribed several medications. The meds made me tired, weak, and sometimes even incoherent. They said I had a nervous disorder and was a paranoid hypochondriac. I endured several psychiatric evaluations because of my lack of concentration and my continuous problems in school.

One of the main problems I had to deal with in school was bullying. I was very small, but my bad attitude kept growing, and the combination of the two got me into many fights. I had also developed a bad attitude and even borderline hatred for the babysitters who always seemed to end up hurting me. Gradually, I hated my Dad too. He was usually not home at night; he stayed out all night drinking in the bars, and I truly resented that.

I often lay awake at night hoping and dreaming that somehow my real Mom and Dad would get back together again. I even hinted to Dad that Mom still wasn't married and that maybe he should call her, but he never did. I suppose Father did know best.

Other nights, I still lay awake scared, hoping, and waiting for Dad to come in and comfort me. Still other times, I fell into a deep, deep sleep, only to be awakened at the last second and rushed off to school in the morning.

I always earned C's, D's, and F's on my report cards and Dad whipped me after almost each one I brought home. I was a very smart kid, and I do remember getting some B's, so I was entirely capable of getting good grades, but the medication the psychiatrists put me on, and the stuff going on at home, made it very difficult to do so.

Becoming Numb to Life

"A family can be the bane of one's existence. A family can also be most of the meaning of one's existence. I don't know whether my family is bane or meaning, but they have surely gone away and left a large hole in my heart."

—Keri Hulme, The Bone People

Chapter 4
Becoming Numb to Life

Eventually, I just became numb to life. I blocked out a great deal of the time between when Sally left and this point in time, but my life at twelve years old was very vivid in my memory. It turned out to be one of the most traumatic years of all.

Dad started going to a doctor who put him on new medications to treat his depression and anxiety. When he came home, he sat down to fill us in on the doctor and the next thing I knew, he fired up a joint right in front of us as he told us about it. Another time, he had been given some "Thai stick," by a friend; it was another plant-based drug just like pot, only about seven times stronger than marijuana. It seemed to relax him, but it also made him act very crazy. As he already had a violent temper and was unstable, this just made the situation even more tenuous.

Within six months of being on these drugs, he had gotten far behind on paying the rent and other bills. My Dad was losing it. In fact, we were all on drugs, except for my two little brothers, and we ate very little except junk food.

It was about this time that Mom came over one day to discuss child support with Dad. It was good to see her, but she didn't bring Lisa. I missed my little sister, but life had pulled us away from one another. In fact, it wouldn't be until twenty-three years later, in 1997, that Lisa and I finally saw each other again.

Mom had brought a bottle of wine with her that day, which was probably not a very good idea because she and Dad were both severe alcoholics. Add that to the fact that my Dad was a drug user with attacks of deep depression, which could be very alarming and violent, and it was a recipe for disaster.

Between his lows, he had incredible high moods, so they started out talking calmly that night and it was nice. I found myself near my mother, but I was scared to death to act as if I missed her. I had become so fearful of Dad that I was incapable of responding to my mother. I desperately wanted to hold her and hug her, but I didn't know how to respond to her without hurting Dad or making him mad.

I felt a lot of anxiety in the room. Dad knew that I wanted to live with Mom, but she wouldn't have it. I could never shake the feeling that I was a bad kid and that it was my entire fault; she didn't think she could handle me. Somehow, everything that went wrong in the family seemed to be my fault, and that seemed to validate my thoughts of killing myself to save my family. I just didn't know how to go about doing it. I was good at stealing, but I didn't know anything about how to kill anything, especially myself.

I always had a soft spot towards other people no matter what they had done to me previously. That night, while they talked, I just couldn't hurt Dad by acting happy and excited to see Mom. I stayed away from her but deep inside, my heart hurt so badly I felt as if I was going to explode with emotion. It was hard, almost impossible to contain it, but in the end, I kept it all in.

After Mom and Dad had drunk about half of the bottle of wine, their tempers flared. The alcohol kicked in, and they began yelling and screaming at each other. I started to shake again; I felt my mind about to snap. I yelled at both of them to stop, but it only got worse. Mom hit Dad

19

several times, and he grabbed her and dragged her down the hallway and into the bathroom, threw her into the shower, and ran the water on her. I think he hit her, but I didn't see it, I just felt it through her screams. I had never felt so helpless.

Dad's drug addiction and alcoholism made him extremely mean. Mom came out fighting, and the apartment manager finally came to the door. The manager argued with Dad, who was late with the rent, and said she was tired of the fighting going on in our apartment. She jammed her finger into my Dad's chest and then he pushed her out the door.

By that time, Mom was bloody, and Dad was all scratched up. I got between them somehow, and without realizing what she did, Mom kicked me in the stomach and sent me flying. That night, the fighting only ended when the police showed up.

My stomach was in knots, and I couldn't go to the bathroom. Two days later, I was in the hospital again. I think I had a nervous breakdown. They had me pumped so full of drugs that I couldn't even think.

Losing My Hero

"I think you have to pay for love with bitter tears."

—Edith Piaf

Chapter 5

Losing My Hero

I was finally sent home to Dad, but by then things had only gotten worse. He didn't seem the same. We were in financial collapse because any money my Dad did make just went towards buying drugs and alcohol. I could feel the stress pressuring him. He didn't sleep much, but then again, neither did I. I didn't go to school during this time because I was always bent over sick, and still had problems going to the bathroom. Looking back, I know my nerves were totally shot.

People from the school came by to check on us, and my brothers told them I was very sick. Dad was either at work or sleeping half of the day. He became despondent and started going off the deep end. He often drank and beat us.

I clung to Brett; he seemed to be the only stabilizing factor in my life. I loved him so much. He always sensed where I was, what I was feeling. He was a comforting presence to me and constantly reminded me that he was my big brother. I felt like he loved me, except when I picked on my little brother. For picking on him, Dad would beat me with a belt. If I ever hit my younger brother, I was hit three times in return.

One day, without any notice, my oldest brother Tim called to say he was coming in on leave from the Marines. Words could not express the joy I felt. I cried when he came through the door. He was big, tall, and built like a rock. It had been a long time since I had felt joy sweep through my life. I was so proud of him!

Drinking that night, Dad was very mean to Tim. He shrugged it off, which seemed to provoke Dad even more. Dad called him a sissy and threatened him. I remember feeling my heart pounding in my chest as I watched.

All the love, joy, and excitement of seeing Tim after all those years were shattered when Dad asked Tim, "Do you think you can take your old man?" At that Moment, Dad charged into Tim, punching him, forcing him to the ground, and putting him in a chokehold. I remember Dad telling him to say "Uncle!" louder and louder, until Tim screamed it.

Tim had thought about fighting back at first, but he knew Dad was explosive and could be extremely dangerous, and he decided not to retaliate. I stood there, horrified, shaking from head to toe when Tim got up crying and walked out of our lives. We didn't see him again for many years. Nobody knew about the pictures I had of him in his dress blues that I cherished so much. Tim was my hero, a United States Marine.

The impact of that Moment permanently filled me with hate for my father. It went deep down into my heart. Although I still loved him with half of my heart, a quarter of it was filled with fear, and the other quarter was now full of hatred. He had shamed my hero in front of my eyes. My need for Dad's love and affection diminished from that day forward.

Nevertheless, not long after that, I found myself once again starving emotionally to make my Dad proud of me, or to get a big hug from him. When he wasn't drinking or involved in his girlfriends, he loved me as best he could. However, our relationship was distorted by his drug and alcohol abuse, and he would turn on me at a moment's notice and whip or hit me in a rage. I could never seem to keep him from getting mad at me. He saw me as a misfit and problem child.

Losing My Purpose in Life

"Heroes are never perfect, but they're brave,
they're authentic, they're courageous, determined,
discreet, and they've got grit."

—Wade Davis

Chapter 6
Losing My Purpose in Life

It was about this time that my life seemed to lose all purpose. I had lost my Mom, my two sisters, my two stepbrothers, and my Marine Corps hero. Things just weren't the same. I went through Dad's ashtray one day, looking for cigarette butts I could shove into his old pipe to smoke. Even though it burned my lungs, the nicotine had become an addiction, a crutch I couldn't do without.

I wandered through the house, looking for something, though I didn't know what. Then I found Dad's loaded gun on his nightstand.

Although I was scared of it, I felt I could obtain a sense of relief by putting it to my head. I sat there thinking of Tim yelling and screaming, "Uncle!" and Mom's bloody face the night she was arrested. I put the gun to my head and felt the cold, steel barrel touch my temple. Fear, and what I perceived to be peace, wrestled in my mind.

Then, I stuck the barrel in my mouth, pointing it up to the roof. Again, I toyed with pulling the trigger. The only thing that kept coming into my thoughts was the sound of Brett's voice.

"Hey, little brother, I love you," I could hear him saying. "Everything will be okay."

Brett was the only one sensitive enough toward me to speak words that made me feel okay about myself and our situation. I began to cry. The memory of Brett's voice was the one thing that prevented me from killing myself that day. I was scared to pull the trigger; I didn't want Brett to find me dead, but I was more than ready to die. I slowly put the gun down and cried at the thought of him finding me that way.

From that day forward, Brett became my Dad, Mom, big brother, and hero. Everywhere he went, I wanted to go. I never told anyone about that day with the gun; I knew the consequences it would bring. I feared the belt because I knew Dad would whip me to the point that I could not walk the next day. Touching his things, especially his guns, would be a serious mistake.

All the years I spent growing up around Dad, I never knew him not to have guns. He never pulled them on us or anyone else, but he didn't have to. He was a Golden Gloves boxing champion in the Navy and was a very dangerous fighter. I remember one time, when I was about eleven or twelve years old, I came home from school with a black eye. Dad was so mad at me that he punched me, called me a sissy, and disowned me. He told me he didn't want a son who couldn't defend himself. Later, he brought me to see one of his friends who was a martial arts instructor and asked him to teach me how to fight.

When I realized I would never win Dad's favor unless I became a good fighter, it set me on a reckless pursuit for the next twelve years to learn how to hurt and maim people. A month never went by without me being involved in at least one fight, usually more. I would do anything to get Dad's approval.

My life was confusing, hurtful, and filled with fear.

About a month after the night Dad threw her in the shower, my Mom filed assault charges, as did the apartment manager. Dad probably had about six assault charges against him by this time, and I never knew of one person who took him down. He was such an explosive fighter and a fast mover that he petrified his opponents. This time was different, however, because these latest assault charges involved women.

Losing My Dad

"All the art of living lies in the fine mingling of letting go and holding on."

—Havelock Ellis

Chapter 7

Losing My Dad

We were in the Dolphin Apartments in Auburn, Washington, when someone knocked on the door. Dad was asleep on his round, white waterbed with his girlfriend. It was sometime very early in the morning, and I was in the living room with Brett.

As Brett answered the door, police officers and a bunch of strangers rushed into our home. They went straight to Dad's room. At first, I couldn't breathe and then I started screaming. Some of the people not in police uniforms grabbed me and put their hands over my mouth. Later, I found out they were from the Department of Welfare and Social Services. The whole apartment erupted into yelling, and more people came storming in. Only seconds had passed, and then they were dragging Dad down the hallway in nothing but his underwear. My little brother Gerald and I were screaming.

Everything was chaos and confusion. I couldn't believe my eyes as they dragged my strong, physically imposing Dad past me helplessly. Dad wasn't a bad man; he loved us, and he did take care of us. I can honestly say that when Dad wasn't drunk or on drugs, he was a loving father. Alcohol can ruin a person's life, making him or her do horrible things, things normally unimaginable, things the person never dreamed of doing, acts so shocking and awful that shame over them nearly kills the individual once sobriety is regained.

Alcoholism and drug addiction are deadly diseases, and destroy the sanity and love of a good home.

I couldn't breathe, and I began to hyperventilate as my Dad was dragged by me. My whole body shook uncontrollably. My mind flashed back to when I was four-years-old, and I watched Mom leave for the last time. I was paralyzed by panic and shivered and trembled with cold fear. I felt like my only hope in this life, my only source of love and whatever flinty, fragile security I had ever known, was being dragged out the front door like a raging wild animal in disgrace. The complete uncertainty of the Moment left me paralyzed. My life was over, it seemed. I could not imagine a future without my Dad.

My twelve-year-old mind was blown. My half-formed, as yet irrational brain was clotted with crazy speculations. I howled in pain. My thoughts had come to a grinding halt. I was choked with feverish questions.

Mom was gone, but Dad had always been there. Now that we didn't have Mom or Dad, what was going to happen? I could not conceive losing both of my parents. What would we eat? Who would pay the rent? Who would buy us clothes for school? Who would put us to bed?

The terrible fear of the unknown suddenly became very real. It was obvious this was disastrous. I didn't know anything about the Department of Welfare or state programs. I was naïve and lost, but I was supposed to be. I didn't even know what a receiving home or a foster home was at that time, let alone juvenile hall!

I wrenched myself from the grip of the social workers and lunged at Dad's legs. I grabbed them and held on with everything I had and screamed, "Don't take my Dad away! He didn't do anything wrong! Don't take him away, please, don't take my Dad away!"

They stopped dragging him and, for a moment, everything seemed to stop. I just knew, in my young mind, that when they saw how much I loved my Dad, they would change their minds and let him stay with us. I just knew they would let him go. Then I felt arms roughly pull me away from Dad again. I started kicking, punching, and fighting for what seemed like my last hope. Strange as it sounds, I never loved Dad more than I did at that Moment.

I couldn't see his face, and I didn't want him to go without me being able to look into his face one more time.

By that time, the workers had me pinned to the carpet, and I was starting to black out. I was breathing, but I wasn't getting any air. My lips and body were numb. People screamed in my face. Men, women, and police officers were all around me. I kept yelling for Dad, but the words weren't coming out of my mouth anymore. Everything seemed to move in slow motion. It was as if someone turned the volume down on television. Everything became muffled, and the noise stopped, then I must have blacked out.

When I opened my eyes, everything was loud again, and I burst out, "My Dad!" My voice was loud again, and I came up off the floor, pulling three or four people with me. I screamed again, "Let me just see my Dad!"

It took what seemed like forever for me to fight my way to the front door jamb. Our door was wide open, and curious neighbors filled the parking lot. Somehow, miraculously, I was able to pull those people who were restraining me and get through the door opening. I looked outside to my right, and I saw the back of Dad's head in a King County sheriff's car backed up into the parking space in front of our apartment.

"Dad! Dad!" I screamed at the top of my lungs.

Several police officers, along with others, forced me back into the apartment. Maybe it was because I am so double-jointed and squirrelly, but I fought so hard that I broke away from them repeatedly. I worked my way outside and almost up alongside him.

At first, I had been fighting out of fear, but then something changed inside me. Anger and hatred that I'd never felt before rose up within me. I didn't strike out at the law enforcement officers because I loved and respected police officers. However, the other people, who were caseworkers from the Department of Welfare, seemed cold and callous. They were adamant about keeping me from Dad.

Then, something snapped inside me, and I began to kick, bite their hands, and punch them viciously. I easily broke their hold on me. I was still screaming for Dad. For a split second, he looked back over his shoulder and struggled to make eye contact with me. We connected for a brief second, but at that moment, the look in his eyes and the expression on his face burned a picture in my mind that has never left me.

As plain as day, his tear-filled eyes said, "I'm sorry, son." Two desperate individuals, who had so much love between them, were torn apart, heading at a breakneck pace toward the unknown.

The caseworkers pinned me to the ground. My body was limp. I had seen his face. I knew it was over. He had the same look on his face that my mother did that day when I was four. Fatigue finally set in and all the adrenaline, desire, and thoughts left my body. I felt a vast emptiness sweep over me. My body seemed to stiffen and then I collapsed from exhaustion and curled up into a ball on the ground.

I don't remember anything about the rest of that day, except that we were placed in a juvenile hall. My body stayed numb all day. I wasn't shaking at all, and I had no fear, which was very unusual. I didn't have peace by any stretch, but I wasn't angry anymore either. It was as if I weren't there. The workers moved me and made me sit or stand, but when they asked me questions, I couldn't speak. I just stared at them and felt nothing. No words formed in my mind, because I wasn't even thinking. I was like a robot. I felt like I had died.

Life as a Foster Kid

"In foster care, it's easier to measure what you've lost over what you have gained, because there aren't many gains in that life and you are a prisoner to someone else's plans for your life."

—John William Tuohy, No Time to Say Goodbye: Memoirs of a Life in Foster Care

Chapter 8
Life as a Foster Kid

There are blackout points throughout my childhood that I believe are not necessarily normal. I believe my mind specifically blocked them out and, overall, that is not necessarily a bad thing.

I seldom, if ever, think back on my childhood. That is probably a very powerful coping mechanism. In fact, while writing this book many years later, I have wept for the very first time over many of the painful things that happened to me, as I've only thought about them again now. I have opened seriously deep wounds that have been sealed shut out of necessity all these years. Most of what I've written has just poured from me. It is a painful process, and I have experienced the same emotions that I lived through back then, all over again.

It was all real; it all happened, and now the pain is still as fresh as if it were yesterday. That's why I've never visited it until now. Reliving an experience for the twentieth time isn't anywhere near as painful and real as living it for only the second time in over thirty years. It is extremely emotional.

The memories have always been there; I've just never chosen to examine them.

I didn't know how many days passed. I was assigned a caseworker. She was a very nice lady who drove a little four-door car. She seemed to care, but she also had many other children on her mind besides me. In fact, she had so many other kids that she forgot about me for six months. The caseworker's huge burden of so many needy kids proved to be another tragedy in my life.

My brothers and I were scattered among different foster homes, but by a miracle, Jay and I were put into the same home in the hills of Endomclaw, Washington.

Our caseworker at the time dropped us off and left. I stood in front of a small, skinny lady, a broad-shouldered man in his early forties and their sons and daughter. I just stood there in shock, trembling. The lady welcomed us into their small, modest home surrounded by a big farm with cows, chickens, and other farm animals. I still couldn't speak, and I stayed that way for the next two weeks. Although nothing came out of my mouth, I obeyed and did what I was told, seemingly without a thought.

During the first two weeks, the people got angry with me, because I wouldn't tell them my name. Jay stepped in and stuck up for me. Jay was a good brother but was quiet and bashful. Because he was usually always the quiet one, he was the one that was abused by our Dad. I never understood why; it was obvious that I was the cause of most of the problems, especially Sally's departure. Still, Jay and I were not as close as Brett and I were.

Many months after being placed into the home, my foster parents told me that my Dad was a bad man. They told me he had been diagnosed with paranoid schizophrenia and hypochondria, declared mentally incompetent, and placed in a medical facility. I heard many scary rumors over the next few years, from our different foster parents and the Department of Welfare people, but I just couldn't and didn't want to believe them. After all, they didn't know Dad as I did.

That first foster home Jay and I were sent to turned out to be a working ranch. The people were paid $112 a month to keep us, so they were making money off us and they made us work the farm. It was a scary time for both Jay and me, filled with fear, forced labor, beatings, and pain that didn't stop for the entire six months.

The father and mother once stood by while their oldest son, who didn't like Jay, beat him until he was bloody. Then their second oldest son beat me until I was also bloody, right in their front yard. Jay was fourteen, and I was only twelve. We were beaten into submission and made to work like dogs on the farm.

Six months later, our caseworker decided to come for a visit. Our foster parents threatened us and told us not to say anything bad. They dressed us up nice and made everything look proper. I was so scared when the caseworker showed up; I could hardly even say hello. She picked up quickly on the fact that there was a problem, and she pulled me outside and sat me in her car. I locked myself in that car and started crying, pouring out six months of torture and grief. The Department of Welfare investigated the home, and it was later shut down from receiving any more foster kids.

Learning to Run Away

"We all flee in hope of finding some ground of security"

—M.T. Anderson, The Kingdom on the Waves

Chapter 9
Learning to Run Away

After that, Jay and I were separated, and I found myself alone in a lady's home. She was an older lady with an attitude, but by this time, I had one of my own.

Her home was a receiving home, a temporary place for kids to stay while in between foster homes. One of the other kids staying there with her had found a .22 caliber rifle and bullets and fired it into a wall in the basement.

I was standing next to him when he fired the rifle, so I spent the next two weeks in the juvenile hall being questioned. By now, my fear subsided and replaced with bitterness and hatred deep down in my heart. I remember crying almost every night for Tim, Brett, Dad, Mom, or my sisters. I felt like I had lost everything.

As I sat there in the youth center, it suddenly hit me that I couldn't think of one thing that I could call mine. I cried hard when I finally realized that I had been stripped of everything, including my innocence and virtue.

The only thing I could find that belonged to me was a sense of shame and guilt. My loss of everything made me angry. I no longer cared about where I was, who I was, or what I did. I guess for very similar reasons, the other boys in there with me at the juvenile hall were hard, calloused, and full of rebellion.

Two weeks in the company of some of them had left a bad impression on me. I had never dealt with rebellion; I had always been too scared to rebel. Now, since I had nothing to lose, I began to strike out at the guards and other people in the welfare system.

"What are you going to do, take something from me?" I yelled, "Like what? What are you going to do, kill me? Go ahead, do it!" Death seemed like a welcome remedy to my constant nightmares, uncertainty, and the crippling sense of loss with which I continually struggled. A normal personality raised in a functional home could never intuitively understand the terrifying insecurity and raging internal anger I had to overcome just to get through the day and to interact sensibly with other people without alarming them or seeming deranged. The energy and concentration required to pass for "normal" were superhuman. What's more, my efforts, as strenuous as they were, were no doubt not wholly convincing to others. I am certain that I frequently appeared very peculiar, if not worse, to most people with whom I came in contact who did not know me or know me well. As for those who did know me, my daily deportment only continued to affirm their wary opinions and assumptions about me, and certainly did nothing to ingratiate me further with them or anyone else.

That is the real tragedy. That's what the trauma of physical and emotional child abuse really does: it creates permanently damaged and disabled people, damaged goods, who silently carry around within themselves megatons of unbearable pain stuffed down deeply inside of them. They have been rendered human time bombs by the abuse they have endured, and without knowledgeable and empathetic intervention, they are doomed. No other word for it. They are misunderstood, incomprehensible, and suspicious individuals incapable of articulating anything to others about themselves or anything else in the world without sounding strange, threatening and dangerous. Minus a miracle or a feat of super-human bootstrapping on the part of the victims themselves, they are fatally wounded people who, lacking the necessary insight, language skills, and confidence to act in their own best interests, are incapable of clearly explaining or expressing themselves. Such poor souls will almost always be an impossible burden on society, will probably die young—and violently.

But I digress. Back to my own story and the takeaway. After a few weeks in juvenile, I was shipped out to another receiving home. As before, I was rigid with tension and fear, not knowing what to expect. On my second day there, the lady informed me that I would be eating liver for dinner. She was at the stove, with her back to me and the other kids. No fan of liver, I rudely popped off to her, cursing, and telling her that I was not going to eat any liver! Without a word, she whirled around from the stove and whacked me hard with the frying pan across the top of my skull. I saw stars and then all went black. She had knocked me out cold. As I blinked and rubbed my eyes when I was coming to and trying to figure out what had happened to me, the evil woman went after me again and again gleefully, with a scary sneer distorting her lips and a deathly malice darkening her eyes. That's when my survival instincts took over, and I jumped up and ran away.

It was that day that I learned the art of running away. I ran and ran and ran from that sadistic woman's house and her disgusting meal of fried liver until I had probably run at least ten miles. Later that day, a police car came by, and the officer hit the brakes when he saw me. I bolted into the roadside bushes out of abject fear, and they leaped out of their cruiser and furiously chased me a long way. Somehow in my fear and desperation, I out-foxed them and got away.

But, mind you: I wasn't actually afraid of the police themselves; in fact, they were the only people who never hurt or abused me and who were really the only people I ever trusted at this time of my life. They only did their job, and they did it well. They never once mistreated me or took advantage of me. In fact, many police officers encouraged me to be strong and optimistic and to overcome my family issues. They tried to reach out to me and give me reassurance and possible routes and solutions that would lead me to a healthy life after the demoralizing mess of a home life that I'd experienced. I have nothing but praise and admiration for the police. They always treated me fairly and kindly. The police always tried to help me.

So, over the next three years, I was placed in no less than twelve different receiving and foster homes, and I was incarcerated (institutionalized) in the youth center six times. I was listed on the police blotter as a runaway perhaps ten times. At that point in my life, when things were really tanking and heading south, I found it easier to run from the authorities and law enforcement than to deal with them. So I just ran and ran, and I never stopped.

Oddly, stupidly, I didn't realize then that running away was only making things much worse for me, only working against me and making my already tough life even more difficult. It was the completely wrong thing to do. In fact, if I had tried, there was nothing else, nothing worse, that I could have devised to make my life harder, more complicated or more impossible to straighten out.

During this time, the courts tried to allow me to live with Mom, who now had custody of my little brother, along with my sister. Although I tried two or three times to live with Mom, it never seemed to work out and always led to me running away or being removed by the authorities. She continued in her alcoholism every day, and when drunk at night she sometimes hit me and beat me, often with such weapons as belts, household and kitchen implements, whatever she could get her hands on that would inflict pain.

Being Abused Becomes a Part of Life

"Childhood should be carefree, playing in the sun; not living a nightmare in the darkness of the soul."
—Dave Pelzer, A Child Called "It"

Chapter 10
Being Abused Becomes a Part of Life

The first time I went to live with Mom, things were uncertain, but the caseworkers and judges were trying to find the best place for me to live. The idea of sending me to live with Mom came up several times, but she worked full time just trying to provide for and manage taking care of both Gerald and Lisa. I was fourteen when the Department of Welfare finally convinced Mom to take me in again. I hadn't known her since I was four-years-old and we'd only had brief and glancing contact since then.

Although Mom was a physically beautiful woman and, when sober, charming and usually pleasant, drinking sometimes destroyed her goodness when she was under its influence and transformed it into malice and a hateful urge to injure and maim her loved ones. She was a non-functional alcoholic who sometimes underwent a total personality change that transformed her into a not so nice person. Typical of those with this problem, she struck out at the most vulnerable, the weakest and those nearest to her. The truth about my mother was her life was ruined and buried inside of a bottle, probably due to her own abuse and the hardships she suffered.

However, I continue to maintain that when she wasn't drinking, she was the kindest, most fun-loving woman in the world, and her company could brighten anyone's life.

She only drank at night and on the days when she didn't work. When she did drink, she sometimes became extremely, almost supernaturally violent, and for some reason, especially violent towards me.

I hated Mom's drinking; it stole away the woman who loved me and who could make me feel safe. Fear and fighting were the norm when she drank. I always likened her to Dr. Jekyll and Mr. Hyde. I loved being with Mom when she wasn't drinking; when she drank, though, she sometimes turned into a completely different person who was dangerously violent and hateful. By now I realized that some of this was due to my own rebellion or bad attitudes that started manifesting themselves in my behavior.

Mom sometimes came after me and beat me, simply because I reminded her of Dad. She always used that one statement as an excuse for her motive. Then, when I'd have a black eye or busted lip the next day, she would innocently ask me what happened. Apparently, she hardly ever remembered coming after me or she was a great actress at the denial of responsibility and embarrassed enough to cover up what she had done. Amnesia was her answer for all her faults and misdeeds.

My Mom kept the scotch, vodka, and soda in many different cabinets throughout the house. Although Lisa and Gerald often came under attack by her, too, during her rages, something about me being so much like Dad really set her off. I remember her once sitting on the couch, staring hard at me. The next thing I knew, she kicked and scratched me, really hurting me and drawing blood.

I never fought back at that time; she was such a strong woman and could easily knock me across the room if she wanted to. I didn't remember ever doing anything to provoke her, but she came after me with incredible hate, and when she beat me, she kept telling me that I was just like Dad. That bothered me so much because I couldn't stop being myself. I felt helpless, indefensible.

47

She must have hated Dad more than anything else in the world. I believe that most of our fighting arose around the subject of him. She tore him down, but I loved Dad. Since I was four years old and she had left, he had been my life and only security, and hearing her deride, malign and tear him down always provoked me to anger and yelling. The older I got, the worse my attitude became.

At this point, I was a very troubled, unstable, and dysfunctional kid. The shaking and fear I dealt with all the time as a child had been replaced with abiding anger and bitterness as I'd grown older. For a long while, it poisoned my life and all of my relationships. Perhaps, because I had heard Dad tear Mom down most of my life, I didn't have the respect for her that I should have had. I had a tremendous amount of love and affection for her, but between Dad's words over the years, which were always ringing in my ears, and her bouts of abusive behavior drinking and beating me, I suppose I wasn't the son I should have been.

Lisa, Gerald, and I hid her alcohol, but when she couldn't find it, she immediately went to the store to buy more. One time, we hid it from her, and she knew what we had done. Although her memory had been affected by her drinking, she remembered that she had just bought some alcohol. The next thing I knew, she was beating me, and I ran outside and all the way down the street to escape. I was used to coming back scared to death of her and waiting until midnight to knock on the window to sneak back in. The next day, everything would be fine. Many times, she did not remember what she had done.

Her abuse put me in the hospital several times. I always covered for her, saying that I had fallen down the stairs or off my bike. I blamed the alcohol and not her because deep down I knew that she loved me. Her drinking, however, ruined any hopes I had of redeeming my childhood love for her.

It was strange to me that, as a four-year-old child, I had felt so safe with her, but at fourteen, I had become scared to death of her.

Because of the constant fear and beatings, I again began to drink myself, just like at Dad's. I poured water into her alcohol to replace what I had taken. Drugs and stealing also again became commonplace activities in my life.

After about four months of this depressing, frustrating routine with Mom, I ran away from her house when she came after me one night. She had clawed my face bloody and bashed me up pretty bad. I had thought of running away many times because of the fighting between us, but this was it. I'd reached my breaking point, the point at which I couldn't take anymore, loving her so much and then being hit and hurt by her. After finally running away from Mom's house this time, I hit a new low and became very despondent. I'd never felt so alone and rejected, but I'd always blamed myself in the end and that often led to me having suicidal thoughts.

After running away this time, I started hitchhiking, and a nice couple picked me up. Because I was so young, they made me tell them what had happened. Although I was fourteen, I still looked like I was only about ten or eleven because I was so small and underweight. After leaving Mom's, my stomach continued to hurt a lot, and I didn't eat much. The couple who had picked me up let me sleep in their car, but I had many nightmares of Mom attacking me in my sleep.

The next morning, I was awakened by the Department of Welfare and was angry that the people who'd picked me up had turned me in. They all wanted me to go back to Mom, but I refused, so I spent a long time in juvenile hall awaiting a new home. While I was locked up, I was plagued with bad dreams.

Then, something wonderful happened. The next home I was shipped off to was the home of the Floberts. They were two very wealthy people, with six or seven foster kids already living in their home. They had a nice swimming pool and a very large home. However, what made this home even more special to me was that it was where Brett had been placed too. I couldn't believe it. I remember crying so hard when I first saw him. Brett had always treated me so well and cared for me. I loved Brett more than anyone else in the world. As it turned out, the Floberts were also very nice people and treated us well.

Nevertheless, the attitude I had developed over the years would eventually get me into deep trouble, and I was arrogant, disruptive, and got into several fights with the other foster kids while I was in their home. I had started practicing martial arts because I was sick of always being beaten up. I wanted to fight back. My attitude was seriously continuing to change for the worse, and the chip on my shoulder grew larger every day.

Seeing Dad Again

"I just let the pain take over, allowing it to numb the pain of being left behind."

—Jessica Sorensen, The Coincidence of Callie & Kayden

Chapter 11
Seeing Dad Again

As things turned out, my brother Brett had been in contact with Dad. Brett had learned that Dad had been in and out of several mental hospitals and was now in very bad shape, in fact, he was psychotic. One day, Brett had me go to work with him and, to my surprise, Gerald and Jay were with him. Without saying a word about it to me beforehand, Brett had planned and connived a way for all of us to get together with Dad.

When I saw Dad's face, I couldn't believe it. It had been years since I'd last seen him in the back of that police car. He was now noticeably older and weaker; his was face ravaged by the years, alcohol and drugs. He was on the run from the authorities who wanted him on so many charges that he had lost count. He was living incognito in California. Seeing us, Dad immediately took charge as if nothing had changed. He instantly went about packing up all of us into the car right then and there, and we recklessly, without any thought of how or where we would live, ran off into the wild blue yonder with him. Eventually, Dad ended up taking us from Seattle, Washington, through Oregon and down into Santa Rosa, California. Wherever we went, it didn't matter to my brothers and me, just as long as we were all together. Even if he was crazy as a loon, certifiably insane, we were overjoyed to be with him. After all, for all his failings, he was our loving and beloved Dad.

When we reached his home in California, we discovered that he had a woman named Trish living with him and that he had been in and out of a wheelchair because of muscle weakness and walking problems. The doctor in California who had started him on prescription drugs for his ailments had accidentally run over him with a GMC truck and bounced him forty-feet across concrete. He was pretty messed up from the accident, and he had become much crazier.

Next, he took us to Oakland, California, where we stayed with some Spanish people and drank tequila with lemon. Dad gave us drugs and alcohol whenever we wanted, and we partied all through the nights. Money was scarce, though, and we went hungry during the first three or four weeks. Dad tried to get food stamps and state assistance; that triggered all kinds of trouble for us and caused the police and Department of Welfare to come in on us. In no time, they found us and took us away from Dad.

The courts put us in a detention center where we stayed locked up for months, awaiting transport back to the state of Washington. Mom was furious about Brett taking Gerald away from her and about our escape to California. Luckily, though, when we arrived back in Washington, Brett and I were placed back into the Flobert's foster home.

Brett was still young, about sixteen or seventeen, when he got married to escape the foster home. He left me, although I begged him repeatedly to take me with him. We were only together for about six months, but it was the longest I had stayed in one place since I was twelve years old.

After Brett was married, he came by to visit me at the Flobert's a lot at first, but between time spent on his work, school, and with his new wife, over a few months, the visits grew fewer and fewer. I felt stripped yet again, and, despite the Flobert's foster home being the best one I'd ever had, I chose to run away. I felt utterly lost and without any hope at all.

I slept in strangers' homes, in the yards of people I did not know, always looking over my shoulder, checking my back, and jittery doing everything, on a panicked run from the police. One night, I even lost all my extra clothes while running from them. I couldn't outrun them carrying a heavy sack of clothes, so I just threw them down, abandoned them and ran away as fast as I could.

Being penniless, absent any resources at all, scared out of my mind, ravenously hungry most of the time, and living outside in the woods exposed to the weather, insects and whatever weirdos happened to wander by was not easy, I can tell you. I vividly remember feeling completely helpless with no clue about what to do next or how to get my life back together. At the same time, I was also dangerously suicidal. The lure of suicide was like a gentle, inviting tide going out and pulling me softly behind it, always whispering my name and seductively beckoning me. Honestly, I don't know why or how I am still here today. The allure of suicide and the final relief it promised was so inviting, almost irresistible in fact, that I am amazed today that I did not succumb to it at the time.

Running away from hurt, pain, and the siren call of suicide, I grit my teeth and hitchhiked a short way down the road to Kent, Washington, which was about twenty to thirty miles from the Flobert's home. I was familiar with the area. There I found an old friend, who was once in a receiving home with me, and who was now living with his Mom and sister in their home. We reconnected like old buds, and he said he'd help me.

I stayed with him for three weeks, but I only slept inside of his home twice. More appealing to me, maybe because it afforded faster and many more alternative escape routes if the authorities showed up, was his tree fort that he'd built in the woods. That shelter and perch on high was much more attractive to me and made more sense. With my friend's encouragement and approval, I quickly settled in and made myself at home in the tree tops. There I sort of slept restlessly each night; that is, slept lightly and nervously because every single bird tweet, cracking twig or passing motorist gunning his engine or screeching his brakes rang my bell and almost gave me a heart attack. Tormented by constant enervating fear, I hated sleeping in the woods. The fact is, I hardly slept at all while there.

Finally, after recognizing the nervous wreck I had become, my friend took me to another house in the neighborhood where he bought three sticks of "Thai stick," the very strong type of marijuana Dad had used. Oh, yeah. I knew all about that mind-numbing substance. So, fueled up and blinded to the idiot stage by this powerful drug, my friend and I spent two days in his tree fort denying the reality of our lives and circumstances, and smoking it like crazy. We smoked it as if there were no tomorrow, smoking it as if our actions had no consequences and whatever we did was not our responsibility. We just couldn't come down. Our will and common sense had been hijacked and rendered entirely ineffectual. Unable to budge, unable to do anything else, anything purposeful or meaningful, we did what we could do; we stayed high and smoked Thai stick until we became totally incoherent and incapable of thought or speech; we eventually lost it—our bodies could only take so much—and we just passed out.

Then, when we woke up intermittently, we'd start smoking it all over again. It was an impossible situation for us.

Somehow, without warning, the cops came into my friend's subdivision looking for me. When I saw them swarming through the underbrush headed for us and clued into what was up, I ran like an Olympic sprinter. However, they ran faster and at last, all of us winded and gasping, they caught up with me on my way toward the highway.

The net result of all this sneaking around and running back and forth was that I was sent back to a life of institutionalization. I was once again incarcerated behind bars in juvenile hall, where I completely lost it. I was raging with anger and almost deranged by what had happened. Wild with anger when the police arrived to arrest me, I resisted arrest in every way imaginable. I was a snarling vicious animal. I yelled, scratched, bit, drew blood, screamed, and kicked, and did my best to break bones. Because of my crazy behavior, I spent my first three or four days in juvenile hall in isolation wearing a white straitjacket.

I hated the thought of suicide, but it seemed the only attractive and appealing solution to the agonizing insecure mess that was "my life."

Like a zombie that had spells of irrational combustible violence, I went grim-faced through several more receiving homes and foster homes, only to eventually explode, totally lose control, and ultimately strike out, hoping to inflict as much pain and damage on others as I could. Always, I would suddenly snap and run away, without warning, sometimes having stayed at any given place for less than two hours. I even stupidly ran to Mom's house once, but that only lasted for a week. It was the second time I had tried to live with Mom, but I knew that plan was going nowhere. That was when I first took a pair of nail clippers with a little file and began cutting my wrist. It started bleeding very badly, but I continued to tear it up. I then moved on to other parts of my body.

Cutting is weird. Only people who have despaired, who have lost all hope and self-esteem, cut themselves. Why do they cut themselves? You would think cutting would hurt and be painful, wouldn't you? But people who do this cut themselves in secrecy, in private, and they take great pains to hide their self-cutting from others—as I did—and they do it to feel better! Somehow hurting themselves relieves them of an unbearable anxiety and hopelessness. Yet the relief from cutting is only temporary. So they become caught in an addictive cycle. The cutting continues, their bodies became wounded and scarred, and they remain mired in shame at what they are doing to themselves and in a deep depression that often ends in suicide.

At any rate, although I instinctively ran once again to my Mom for safety and refuge, inside I already knew my Mom couldn't keep me. As much as I loved her and wanted more than anything to be with her, my Mom was personally and psychologically incapable of giving me a loving home because of her hopeless alcoholism and violent tendencies when drinking. What's more, maybe as a result of the amount of alcohol she was consuming, she was also mentally incapable of understanding her problems and so was powerless to do anything to fix them.

Whatever the case, the authorities had ruled on this. I didn't have legal permission to be with her, and, by law, she would have to turn me in. I certainly didn't want to go back to juvenile hall in Seattle; it was like a prison. Sad to say, but at the time and under the conditions, cutting my wrists seemed to provide the only relief available to my crippling, sleepless anxiety, and became the only way I endure this unbearable, confounding situation.

I continued to cut myself over the following days and weeks, trying to sort it all out. I grew weaker and weaker and took a bunch of Mom's pills to ease the pain. It hurt a lot, but it didn't seem to be killing me very fast.

Even so, I kept it up like an obsessive-compulsive nutcase, like the addict I was, for the benefit of the brief relief it gave me from my uncontrollable panic attacks.

I had no idea what would happen as a result. Frankly, I did not expect any health repercussions, serious injury or damage to come from this self-destructive habit of mine. I was surprised when I woke up one morning, confused and out of it, in the hospital with a terrible stomach ache and I did not know why. It was more than just puzzling, because once more, I was wearing a white straitjacket.

In the System Again

"Running away was easy; not knowing what to
do next was the hard part."

—Glenda Millard, A Small Free Kiss in the Dark

Chapter 12

In the System Again

The Department of Welfare was there at the hospital when I woke up
again in a straight-jacket, not Mom. I now had a new caseworker, my third
or fourth one. Like all the rest of them, her job and only interest was to
quickly find me another home. She wasn't interested in me or my story.
None of the caseworkers ever seemed to care about me. Perhaps it was an
occupational hazard for them to become numb and indifferent to abuse
and impoverishment. But maybe they just really didn't have the necessary
time to get involved and feel their feelings. I admit that they were always
overwhelmed and swamped by desperate cases of abused, needy kids who
needed a safe place to live. I can't say I blame them. I was just another
pathetic case; I was only number 0006743 in the system.

My caseworkers were never personal with me, either. They never
really connected or empathized. They never once became emotionally
involved or reached out to me. As young and naïve as I was back then, it
was still obvious to me. It would be obvious to any impartial observer that
it was just a job to them. They were only going through the motions. I
never got close to any of them, including the odd one that did seem to care
a little bit for me. They would just stick me in a home, fill out the
paperwork, and then disappear as if they had never been there in the first
place.

After leaving the hospital, I was immediately sent back to the juvenile
hall. Eventually, I went through two or three more bad foster homes before
I turned fifteen. I stayed on the run a lot, hiding from the police and

authorities, and I often went back to my old foster homes to get money or to see people. I went to some of them for solace or money, only to have cops storm into the foster home and catch me five minutes after I had arrived. My helplessness to improve my situation made me feel awful and worthless.

I looked up to my brother Brett, and so I searched around for him and finally located him, but Brett would only let me stay with him for a couple of days. Strangers sometimes took me in for a night or a weekend but always dropped me back off on the interstate, eager to get rid of me.

I became exhausted and demoralized from always being consumed with anxiety, always running and always looking over my shoulder like a criminal. At night I cried, sometimes hard. Sometimes all night long. I desperately missed my family. Their absence was an aching, gaping hole in my stomach. It made me feel physically sick and weak. It was incapacitating. I thought of all my losses, I could not help but constantly ruminate on them, but I tried only to remember and focus on the good times. When I was hurting or missed my family the most, I took whatever drugs I could get my hands on, and I drank like a fish. Sometimes, though, when I had no money, I had to fight the sickening confusing hurt inside of me unaided, stone cold sober, which was nothing less than agony.

I saw myself as repugnant, socially unacceptable, and clearly the absolute dregs of society. I was sure I was an outcast because I deserved to be, it was clearly my own fault, and because I had no redeeming qualities. I mean, if my own mother hated me and thought that I was worthless, I darn sure must be worthless, right? I felt like a wanted criminal because no one liked me or wanted to have anything to do with me. When feelings like this got the upper hand and overwhelmed me as I walked down the highway, I would almost throw myself into the oncoming traffic. It would have been so easy and then everything, all the hurt and pain, would be over. Somehow, I never did, though, because I was too afraid that the oncoming traffic wouldn't kill me, but would only end up paralyzing me and maybe put me in a wheelchair for life. I could not take a chance on that happening. Totally disabled and penniless was not something to aspire to in my book.

I missed Gerald and Lisa terribly, so at last I caved into the pain of their absence from my life and I called Mom. She was not at all receptive in any way to my pleas and she refused to take me in as a runaway, so I called my caseworker from a pay phone, willing to turn myself in if she would let me live with Mom again. It was all I could do. I was at a complete loss and my nerves were in shreds. It took a good while to convince my caseworker and to push all the paperwork through the bureaucratic system. And I was in no way overjoyed that I had to stay in the juvenile hall again, but at least I got a warm bed and three meals a day there.

Being on the run and sleeping in the woods had really gotten old and drained me. Even though juvenile hall did give me a bed to sleep in and food, I still hated being locked up. The kids in there were mean and ugly to me. I had to watch my back all the time and be hyper-vigilant. Every time I turned around, I was fighting somebody off.

Over the years, out of this paranoid necessity for constant self-defense, I practiced and forced myself to use my martial arts. Eventually, because of my discipline and adherence to a rigorous training routine, I had become very good at effortlessly hurting people. When someone called me "shorty" or "stupid," I reflexively lashed out and fought him or her. I felt myself getting meaner and meaner. I exploded with a terrible rage as I had them pinned on the ground with my hands around their throats. When they saw my face against theirs, their eyes bulged, and I could see their fear. I knew they must have seen the result of all the years of anguish, fear, and hatred in mine.

When I fought, I took everything out on my opponents. I was implacable and unmerciful. Today I hang my head thinking of those times, and I'm ashamed of how brutal I was back then. Yet before I could ever really hurt anyone in a fight, a soft spot inside of me stopped me and held me back. I would always let up and let them go before I had done any serious harm. It was strange, but I had carried that soft spot of compassion inside of me, even as a tiny little boy, and it never allowed me to kill, seriously injure or put anyone to the point of death, except myself.

Alcohol Finally Destroys My Relationship with Mom

"A man who drinks too much on occasion is still the same man as he was sober. An alcoholic, a real alcoholic, is not the same man at all. You can't predict anything about him for sure except that he will be someone you never met before."

— Raymond Chandler, The Long Goodbye

Chapter 13

Alcohol Finally Destroys My Relationship with Mom

The authorities finally let me go to Mom's house to live after my case lagged in the system for months on end. I wanted so much to see it work out between us this time, for everything to be loving and peaceful, but unfortunately, at just that time Mom's drinking and the terrible toll it was taking on her behavior was at its worst. She was a dangerous alcoholic and capable of anything. She was what they call a thirsty drinker and guzzled a full fifth of scotch whiskey in only three hours. When she was drunk, it almost seemed as if she deeply hated me and wanted me dead. Aware of this, and devastated by it, I tried to stay clear of her when she was drinking, sometimes hiding down in the basement for hours or days on end.

Back then, maybe because I only ate irregularly and then not much, I only weighed about ninety pounds, so I was still very small. That meant I didn't stand a chance against Mom's size and strength. Anyway, I had lived there just a short time before I was doing drugs and drinking booze all the time to cope with the terrible stress and fear of unpredictable, explosive violence in the house.

I don't remember exactly how long I lived with Mom this third time, but I do remember one specific horrible night.

Mom had been drinking heavily that night and had gotten into a loud and nasty verbal fight with her own mother. Although it was a commonplace occurrence between them, this time, it put Mom in a very bad dark mood. Mom's fight with her mother made her so angry that it caused her to drink even more. That night I learned, bit by bit, from things she let slip, that one of her sisters had previously committed suicide, and later that her other sister had done the same. I was shocked. Her two sisters' suicides certainly explained a lot about Mom's erratic, mean behavior. Both of these tragedies suggested a genetic mental problem, probably clinical depression, in her family which Mom could have inherited.

My Mom had also lived a very difficult life apart from her sisters' suicides, which was what, I believe, led to her serious addiction to alcohol. Not only was I psychologically damaged, but my mother's own story was similar to mine, especially the abuse she suffered from my Dad. Because I was so young at the time, I never knew all the facts of her painful life, except that her mother was also abusive, both physically and verbally, to all of her kids. This particular night, however, would prove to be another very painful memory from my childhood that I have never been able to shake.

Mom was upset because I had done something that reminded her of Dad; being like him got me into so much trouble with her. She went on a rampage. At that moment, I believe she thought I was Dad.

As she began to kick and punch me, I did what I normally did, which was ball up and cover my face as best I could. Sometimes I grabbed a pillow off the couch to help protect me, but it normally didn't do much good. I screamed back at her, but she wouldn't stop. She ripped the hair from my head.

As I lay there beaten, with my heart hurting, I was getting angry. I knew it wasn't her fault, but the alcohol had taken over her mind, and all the hatred that she had for Dad was lost on me. That's when I made a tragic mistake — I fought back, as I had never done before. I pushed and kicked her off me.

Mom just stopped in shock. She couldn't believe what I had done. I will never forget the way the anger just exploded across her face.

She said something like, "How dare you!"

I wasn't sure what she was about to do, but my body was gripped with fear from the top of my head to the bottom of my feet. She looked around as she cursed me and abruptly turned toward the fireplace. She grabbed a poker and turned toward me. I jumped off the couch, only to jump right back as she swung the poker at me. She hit me across the shoulder, and the pain was incredible. She stumbled and fell on me. When I felt her fingernails dig into my face, I began to push and kick as hard as I could.

Every time I thought about hitting her, though, I couldn't bring myself to do it. I cried uncontrollably because I was fighting back, but I was afraid of hitting her. I never hit Mom; something about her did not permit me ever to do that. I loved her, and I understood that she was not herself now.

We both fought on, and she grabbed me by my throat. I had both of my hands on the poker now, and she had one hand on my neck. Because she was so drunk, she had a hard time keeping her balance, which gave me just enough edge to keep her from seriously hurting me with the poker.

I was scared; I felt like I was struggling for my life. This fight was, by far, the worst fight we had ever had. I remember asking myself, "Why did you have to fight back?" There was no stopping her now. I had fought back, and she was furious with me. No matter how much she kicked, punched, or scratched me, it didn't seem to slow her down.

I gasped and choked from her hand around my throat. I was so worried about the poker that I didn't realize that I had lost my peripheral vision. Everything to the sides of me was going black and was closing in. I started seeing stars. I had never felt this way before, and I panicked. I kicked, pushed, and screamed, but Mom had me pinned to the couch, and wasn't letting go of my throat. I couldn't take my hands off the poker. It took both of my hands, against her one, to keep the poker from hitting me, so I didn't have a free hand to use to get her hand off my throat. I felt just like I did the first time I was put in a straitjacket and couldn't get out.

I was overcome with an incredible fear and when I thought of that straitjacket, I finally exploded. I pushed Mom to one side, moving out from underneath her and to the right. I got up, but so did she. She pulled back the fire poker to hit me and without thought or warning, I punched her in the face with everything I had in me. She was knocked back, fell over the coffee table, and hit the floor.

I screamed, petrified as I realized that she was unconscious. I knew that my punch alone didn't knock her out. Her fall to the ground, along with the alcohol, had probably made her pass out. I couldn't believe what I had done. I felt fear and shame, along with a sense of relief. I quickly realized that I had been more scared of that poker than I had been of hitting Mom, although I wasn't sure if that was good or bad. I just knew that for right now I was safe. She couldn't hit me while she was unconscious.

It was only then that I became consumed with fear by another thought, "What if she wakes up?"

I grabbed the poker and hid it underneath the couch. I became as afraid of her waking up, as I was of seeing her lying there. Mom fell and passed out a lot when she drank, but sometimes only for a short time. My punch wasn't strong enough to hurt her; in fact, I don't even think I connected well, which was a partial relief to me.

As I tried to prop her head up into a better position, I noticed that she had blood on her. I didn't want to make her too comfortable for fear of her waking up. I just didn't like her head being in that position as she lay there partially wrapped up in the coffee table. I wiped the blood off of her and was scared that she had cut or hurt her head during the fall. It was then that I realized the blood was dripping from me. My face was bleeding, my nose specifically, and I had blood all over my shirt. I couldn't feel any pain. I was numb with fear.

I did not want to be in the house when she woke up.

I grabbed the phone, dialed 911, and told them my Mom and I had gotten into a bad fight. They were familiar with our names and situation since Mom had beaten me in the past. The lady wanted me to stay on the phone and talk to her, but Mom moved, looking like she was about to wake up. I bolted out the front door, ran down the block, and jumped into the bushes. I couldn't believe how scared I was. I was scared that I'd hit her. Scared of where I'd have to go now.

I started to run, but as the numbness left, I felt the pain all over my body. With every passing minute, I hurt more. Suddenly, I saw police lights coming down the street, followed by a fire truck, more police, and an ambulance. I wanted to run, but if I did, I couldn't see Mom and I had to make sure she was okay. Besides, with the police there, I knew she wouldn't be able to hurt me.

As I walked back up into our yard, I became extremely weak and dizzy. Mom had scratched me all over my arms, chest, and face, so I was covered with blood. As I walked up, one of the cops took one look at me and said, "Oh, my God."

They all quickly gathered around me, and that was when my legs finally gave out. The grass was wet and felt cold. I don't remember anything else after that, except telling the police what had happened. I don't remember where I was at the time. I didn't tell them about the poker, but it had left a long, skinny red mark across my left shoulder.

I ended up in the hospital and stayed there for a long time. I looked at pictures placed in front of me and underwent many psychological tests.

Being Sent Away

"For there to be betrayal, there would have to
have been trust first."

—Suzanne Collins, The Hunger Games

Chapter 14
Being Sent Away

Mom came to see me in the hospital, and it was a very scary visit. She acted sober, but I could tell by her demeanor that she'd had something to drink. She talked very firmly to me, and I could tell she was angry inside. I felt that I had stepped over the line with her, and she had put up a wall between us. She didn't want to hug me or kiss me. She had no remorse for what happened and was in complete denial. She made me feel like I had attacked her, and couldn't be allowed to do that again. I felt so bad for fighting back, especially for hitting her. I seriously cringe even to think about it today.

Her visit was short, and I knew something was wrong. I had never before felt a wall like that between us. She told me she had signed papers for me to go away and she acted very strange, indifferent, and somehow satisfied with herself as if she had gotten revenge. I had never had a meeting like that with Mom; it was more like a business meeting than a mother and son visit. She acted like a caseworker, and I didn't feel like the words she spoke were coming from her. She turned around and left; she never kissed or hugged me goodbye.

At fifteen years of age, I didn't comprehend what had just happened to me. I soon found out that Mom had told the authorities I had assaulted her, and all the scratch marks I had on my body were caused by me, not her. Labeled as a dangerous person, I was instantly compared to my psychopathic father. This brought swift judgment.

I was hauled off to a boys' correctional facility, named Boysville, located in Yakima, Washington, near Walla Walla State Prison. I didn't realize I was being locked up until I arrived. After being sentenced to one year there, I felt something inside me had died. That next year was terrible.

I fought, I was locked up, was abused, lonely, and confused. I contemplated suicide many times. After unsuccessfully cutting my wrists, and then having my stomach pumped the last time, it didn't seem so easy. Besides, in Boysville, we were under constant supervision, with someone around watching us like a hawk twenty-four hours a day.

There were approximately sixty to eighty boys in Boysville. It was a very long year for me. Most of the boys there were really tough customers, full of anger and bitterness, quick to take offense and strike out. Although we, the inmates, planned and tried to execute several escapes, we were always caught and punished. Anyway, at least a hundred miles of desert road surrounded us in every direction, making it nearly impossible to ever really escape.

The officers and administration told me they would rehabilitate me, but I didn't know from what. Everything I had done in my life that had gotten me in trouble was a result of my being in a life-threatening situation and involved my desperate attempts to survive and save my own life. Of course, to outsiders who could not possibly understand, my fighting and violent behavior, as well as my constant running away from the foster homes and my Mom's home, looked like pure unbridled rebellion and a total disrespect for the law and the rights of others. Yet they were actually nothing more than my last-ditch efforts to save my own life. After what

I'd been through in my terminally dysfunctional childhood home, I had become constantly hyper-vigilant, on guard and just trying to survive.

To get along at Boysville, I made up stories about why I had been sent there. Many of the other kids locked up with me had been sent there for things like rape, grand theft, selling drugs, robbery, etc. I came to the conclusion I was sent there because I was just too hard to handle. I had issues with authority and lacked self-control and discipline. When it came down to it, I really didn't understand exactly how or why I was there at all, except that Mom had lied to the courts, telling them that I'd attacked her, and had signed papers to put me away.

After the year at Boysville, I was released back into my mother's custody. Barely a month after my return, things were right back where they used to be, with the same beatings, as she continued to drink herself into a crazy violent state, and tell me how much I was just like Dad. I resolved that I would never hit her again, even if she killed me. The guilt I carried around during that year in Boysville was worse than death, and I couldn't go through it again.

When things got bad at Mom's this time, I ran outside, or down into the basement trying to evade the dangers of the situation. The constant psychological stress took a heavy toll on me during those months back at Mom's and eventually I was grasping for any way out of the nightmare. I had no money or resources of my own, so it was clear that, to get away from the hell on earth with Mom, I needed an income, and that meant I needed a job. I dropped out of school, and after a lot of searching, I finally got my first job cleaning windows on high-rise buildings. I immediately took to it and was good at it. It turned out to be a life-changing event.

The work required that I scale tall buildings of forty or fifty stories up, feats that scared the daylights out of my boss. I belted without rope the front side of the Ivers Smith Tower, which was forty-three stories high and cleaned all the windows on the building in six days, record time. I also completed a seventy-six-story bank building at a record pace. Nobody understood why I took all those chances and why I seemingly had no fear of the obviously dangerous occupational hazards inherent in the work.

The truth is, all the fear I had faced throughout my childhood was much greater than stepping off a high-rise building. Getting that job helped me gain confidence, an absolute necessity to getting ahead in life. I loved climbing the buildings, and cleaning the windows was something I quickly found out not everyone could or would do for any amount of money.

Mom didn't stop drinking, though, and she came after me again one night. I got away from her, fled the house, and I ran until I was picked up by the Seattle police and put back in juvenile hall. This time, I was put in front of a judge. It was then that I realized that I had been pulled out of the Department of Welfare's jurisdiction. The judge read the records of the many foster and receiving homes in which I'd been placed, and my habit of always running away from them. He disapprovingly reviewed my record of time spent in correctional facilities. Then he asked me why I was such a problem child.

"I'm not a problem child!", I snapped back. That remark and the disrespectful tone in which I made it didn't go over very well with him. I had finally convinced myself that I was only a part of the problem, but now I was suddenly standing in front of a judge who was telling me I was the whole problem.

Without thinking, or fully realizing his authority, I got very angry and vented to the judge about how the system had ruined my life. He fired back, telling me that I was clearly a menace to society and that I would never amount to anything. Then he slammed down his gavel and emancipated me as a minor at sixteen years of age.

By making that ill-advised retort to the judge, I had just lost my first real job, one that I loved — and my car and any chance I had of living in a real home. I was bereft of everything.

They took me outside, placed me on a city bus, and I rode it all the way into Chinatown. I had no money, no clothes, nothing. I was scared of the prostitutes, gang wars, and the shootings downtown. That year was a cold winter in the northwest, and I slept in the snow on the streets of Seattle. I had never been so cold in my life. I thought of throwing rocks through windows so I could be arrested and sent back to juvenile hall. At least there, I would be warm and get something to eat.

However, as it would turn out, my life was about to take a turn for the worse.

Living on the Streets

"We think sometimes that poverty is only being hungry, naked and homeless. The poverty of being unwanted, unloved and uncared for is the greatest poverty."

—Mother Theresa

Chapter 15

Living on the Streets

As a sixteen-year-old boy, I started a life on skid row that would last for the next year-and-a-half. The hardship, loneliness, shame, guilt, fear, and pain I endured during that time drove me to the lowest point of my life. Nothing could have prepared me for life on skid row. It was a hard and very lonely way for a sixteen-year-old kid to live.

I learned very quickly from a wino where to give blood to get ten dollars. I had to give him half of my money for showing me where to give blood, but the information was worth it.

After donating blood, I went to a little restaurant, where I ordered a hamburger and French fries. They tasted so amazingly good, but I was so hungry that it didn't even come close to filling me up. I only had about sixty cents left, so I hit a bubble gum machine and got two mouthfuls of gum, which helped curb my appetite.

I met a beautiful girl who was also a runaway and looking for money. I didn't know it at the time, but this was my first encounter with a prostitute. We walked together, trading stories and it felt nice to talk to someone. Soon, a man pulled up and she hopped in his car. I could see them negotiating through his window, but I had no idea what was going on. They were gone in a flash. I was so naïve.

I ended up fighting with the bums on the street, and after only a week, no one talked to me anymore. I was dirty, and my clothes were smelly from sleeping in dumpsters. People who walked toward me turned around and sometimes walked on the other side of the sidewalk. Some people looked right into my eyes, and I felt something from them as if they were concerned for me, but most people pretended they didn't see me. It was as if I were invisible, or wasn't real.

I remember once standing at a stoplight, waiting to cross the street in downtown Seattle during lunch. The streets would fill with businesspeople, and as I stood there surrounded by others, I tried to look into their faces, but no one would look back at me. I could tell that I made them uncomfortable. I felt rejected by them. Rejection by the loved ones in my life hurt, but having strangers reject me didn't affect me.

"Hey kid, what are you doing out here?"

That was the usual response if I approached someone else on the street. Some of them called me "little man." The other people living on the street were usually nice to me, especially if I had money. Drinking with the winos became one of my primary activities during the first few months that I lived on the streets. Those who looked upon me would probably have called me a wino as well, although I never considered myself one. We bummed money, bought a bottle of wine, and sat on the park benches getting drunk, laughing, and carrying on, while always watching out for the police.

During the first month or so, I was stopped by police officers downtown frequently, but after a while, they didn't bother me anymore. They radioed my name in, without any identification, and let me go. I did purchase a fake I.D., but it didn't work when I tried to buy liquor, even though it said I was twenty-one. All the other bums were older, though, and the people in the stores knew them all by name.

I became known as the "money man." No one could get money as I could. I learned to go to the Salvation Army to shower and get some food, but they only let me stay for one night at a time. The bums showed me two or three places where I could go, and I alternated around them two or three times a week, so I could get a meal and sleep on their floors. That wouldn't buy liquor, but it allowed me to shower and pick up some secondhand clothes.

Between 3:30 and 6 p.m., I hit upper-Seattle and could collect between fifteen and thirty dollars. I looked sad, telling people my Mom had forgotten me and that I needed money for bus fare to get back home. People gave me their change and sometimes even a dollar. Some just ignored me, while others called me a liar.

I found that the younger I acted and the more scared I looked, the better my chances were of getting some money. People started to recognize me and remember my story, so I had to remember what story I told them or just keep changing locations.

After I had made my money for the day, I met up with other bums later in the evening. We put all our money together and bought bottles of rum, whiskey, or wine. They drank a lot of cheap wine, and it tasted awful. Nevertheless, it made all my hurt disappear so that nothing would matter for the next six hours or so. It also warmed my stomach, and I'd stop shaking from the cold. Then, I'd crawl into a garbage dumpster, surround myself with newspapers and fall asleep.

I carried a knife for protection and practiced stabbing at things with my umbrella, in case someone tried to hurt me. I twirled that umbrella around my body and dared anyone to mess with me.

Kidnapped in China Town

"I am no bird; and no net ensnares me: I am a free human being with an independent will."

—Charlotte Brontë, Jane Eyre

Chapter 16
Kidnapped in China Town

One day, as I walked through Chinatown, I saw two Chinese guys giving a lady a hard time. By this time, I knew what a prostitute looked like and what they did. Although none of them paid any attention to me, I could tell this lady was in trouble.

They argued and yelled at her, and I walked right up to them, twirling my umbrella as I said in a threatening voice, "Hey, what do you think you're doing?" Both of the men immediately jumped on me and threw all kinds of kicks and punches at me. Apparently, both guys were experienced martial artists, because I was getting a beating I'd never forget.

Toward the end of the fight, as I lay face down on the concrete, one of them took my umbrella and twice thrust it into my back. The metal point, originally blunt, was now sharp because I had spent several hours grinding it on concrete curbs and fashioning it into a weapon.

The first stab pierced my upper left side. The second stab, directly in the center of my back, was much worse because it hit my spinal column.

I could hardly walk as they led me away with a choker chain. I remember looking back at the girl I had attempted to help, but no feelings showed on her face. It was almost as if I hadn't even tried to save her.

How could she be oblivious to the fact that I had just been badly beaten and stabbed, trying to help her? They forced me to be their slave around Chinatown for two days. Both of them were mean and repeatedly hit me on my head or face with their open hands. Finally, I got up enough nerve to plan an escape.

Because I was so petrified of them, they had no idea I was about to run. They also didn't know that when my adrenalin kicked in, fueled by fear, I could run like a bolt of lightning.

As I planned my escape, fear built up in my body when I thought of them catching me. But the longer I was with them, the less they watched me. All I needed was for neither of them to look at me for five seconds, and I would be gone.

Looking back, I realize they were either loan sharks or part of the Chinatown mob, because they collected money from each store owner, forcing them to pay up. They must have also pimped several prostitutes since they stopped to hand money to them. They liked to hit me in front of their clients, so they could see the fear grip my body. My fear reaction seemed to add to their feeling of power and invoked a corresponding fear in the faces of store owners.

Once, they took me into a little shop, which may have been a restaurant that sold Chinese stuff. As they walked in, they started looking at people and speaking Chinese. Again, I started to count the times they watched me. In five minutes, I had gotten as much as ten to fifteen seconds between looks. As they became very involved with negotiations with several people, I knew this was going to be my chance. The more I thought of going through the exit door, the more fear built up inside of me. I waited until the moment I felt as if my body was about to explode.

I slowly opened the door, and then bolted like lightning, clearing a city block in less than five seconds. I ran hard into the alley, and jumped into a big garbage dumpster, burying myself into the trash. I covered myself with empty boxes so they wouldn't see any of my body if they looked inside. I knew that if they found me in that alley all alone after escaping them, they would kill me.

I stayed in the dumpster all day and almost all night until I finally mustered the courage to sneak out in the darkness. It was about two or three in the morning. I ran out of the alley and never stopped until I was out of Chinatown and halfway into downtown Seattle.

For many weeks after that, I stayed around the corner of First and Pike Streets, or Jackson and Union Streets, near a donut shop where I felt safe. The shop owner's name was Gunther.

Two police officers, one with red hair, patrolled about a six-block radius. Once or twice each week, someone was stabbed or shot. The two police officers were nicknamed Batman and Robin. Some people liked them; others didn't. I tried to make friends with them since I felt safe in their presence, but they refused to talk.

Downtown Seattle was much rougher than Chinatown, running full blast nightly until around three or four each morning. I was scared being downtown, at the heart of crime, with strip joints and prostitutes on every corner. When I looked into the faces of the people, I saw so much evil and hatred.

However, during the day when there were no prostitutes or bad guys, the area underwent a miraculous change. The Pike Place market filled with shoppers, visitors, and many decent people. Although the dirty peep show places and some of the XXX theaters still ran during the day, the majority of the daytime people were shoppers, visitors, and business people.

I hated nights in Seattle. Everyone had a scam or some evil lurking up his or her sleeve. Drugs, prostitution, and robbery ran rampant, as did fights in the clubs, which brought cops rushing in from nowhere. I often ran and hid out of fear when this happened, even though I hadn't done anything wrong. I really struggled living on the streets. Although I tried to act tough and talk big, I was still a scared little twelve-year-old boy living in a sixteen-year-old body. I ran scared all the time, but I couldn't put my finger on the exact source of my fear.

The Streets Took a Toll on Me

"It was a source of both terror and comfort to me then that I often seemed invisible — incompletely and minimally existent, in fact.

—Marilynne Robinson, Housekeeping

Chapter 17

The Streets Took a Toll on Me

I tried to find a job downtown at any of the janitorial companies around, but no one would hire me without a place of residence, a driver's license, a phone, and real skills. I had none of the above.

I was broke, hungry, and depressed. I just stood on the street and watched people walk by. Everyone was in his or her little world. No one knew me or knew anything about me, and no one cared. I might as well have been invisible. I was about to go to sleep in a garbage dumpster again that night, hungry, alone and afraid. That was when I finally lost it.

I shocked myself when I just exploded and began to scream at complete strangers walking by oblivious to my situation, "Don't you care? I have nothing! They took my family! Doesn't anybody care? Can't you see me?"

As I stood on the street corner screaming, about forty or fifty people just stopped and stared at me. When I finished, I just stopped and began to cry. When I looked into people's eyes, I could see that some of them wanted to help. Many of the women, especially, seemed to look on me with compassion or pity, perhaps because of their maternal instincts, but they also looked somewhat afraid of me. At that point, I could not say that I blamed them.

The faces of a few men showed compassion too, but no one had anything to offer me. As I stood there looking at them looking at me, I felt as if they were just as lost as I was.

Suddenly feeling very embarrassed, I ran into an alley, slumped down against a wall, and sobbed. A few minutes passed, and I had just started to get myself back together, when two men, one black and one white, approached me. They looked around as they walked up to me and the black guy pulled out a big knife, one of those fancy switchblades and snapped it open in my face.

I couldn't believe it. Look at me! I had nothing! Absolutely nothing! And I was excruciatingly aware of how poor my chances were of getting out of the hopeless morass I had created of my life. I had pretty much given up on everything at this point, but now these two guys wanted to rob me? Give me a break! They must be crazy or jonesing for drugs and alcohol so badly they couldn't recognize a hopeless loser when they saw one!

The black guy with the knife told me to "give it up. We know you're hustling," he said, "and we're taking over this operation. Now pay up."

I jumped to my feet and screamed all over again. I pulled my pockets inside out and yanked my shirt up around my neck so he could see I had nothing of value, not even anything worth the two bucks it would take to buy a rotgut bottle of wine.

My bizarre behavior had an effect. When I did that, I seemed to have provided them a convincing demonstration of how a dangerous psychopath would behave. Suddenly, both guys' bloodshot eyes got as big as saucers, and in a flash, they wheeled around and bolted like lunatics themselves out of the alley down the street. Giving no thought to what I was doing and whether it was safe, I raced after them, waving my fists in the air, cursing, yelling and screaming at the top of my lungs. It was bedlam. I chased them up to the street corner. At the street corner, I stopped and watched as they kept on sprinting straight on through to the next block.

As they disappeared into the distance, and I stood there in shock over what I had done, another guy pulled up alongside me in a car and asked me if I wanted a ride. I turned my back on him and walked back down to the alley. He followed me and tried to get me into his car again.

"You stupid weirdo! Get out of here!" I screamed. "You're sick, and I'm going to call the police on you!" He punched the gas and got out of there quick! That's when I started shaking all over and felt as if I was going to snap.

I was hungry, cold, and broke, and it just wasn't fair. I went into the alley and dug through the dumpster. I found some old, stale donuts and some other food that had been thrown away. I ate it, found some newspapers and cardboard to sleep on, crawled in the dumpster and began to cry. It was a very cold night, so I stayed inside the dumpster and closed the lid. It made everything quiet and stopped the wind from howling inside. I felt safe inside that garbage can. It stank, it was uncomfortable, and I was still freezing cold, but at least I wasn't being abused.

Dreams of my family during the times when we were all together tormented me during the night. It was impossible for me to get my mind off the horror of my situation. The more I tried, the more I cried. I craved drugs or alcohol, anything to help me escape reality, anything to take away the pain I felt. As I lay there in the dumpster, I suddenly thought back to the black guy carrying the knife.

That's when the realization hit me, "Oh my God! He could have killed me! I could be dead right now!"

I remembered watching his eyes getting bigger and bigger and fear spreading across his entire face as I jumped up and screamed at him. Suddenly, picturing the scene, I laughed aloud alone inside that stinking dumpster. I had scared that creep, and he was the one with the knife. The mental picture of him running away from me unarmed like that made me laugh so hard simply from the insanity of it all.

Then, I started to talk out loud to myself about how absurd it all was, but I stopped when I realized I had no one to tell this funny story to. After that, the inside of my dumpster fell very quiet. At times like this, the silence and my loneliness were what I hated the most. I had no one to talk to or to share either my pain or joy with. Waves of despair and a deep sense of being alone flooded over me. Once again, I cried and moaned pointlessly in the smelly solitary darkness of that nasty dumpster. Now I was really frustrated – yet not tired enough to sleep – so I lay awake in the lonely dark and mulled over my depressing situation, growing more depressed and hopeless with every passing second.

There in the darkness of the foul-smelling dumpster that served as my shelter, I tried to consider where I would be in five years, and where I could be in five years, if I truly applied myself, worked hard and had some lucky breaks. But my imagination choked and failed me. I did not have a shred of inner optimism left. All hope had deserted me. However hard I tried, my future looked as bleak as my present bed, and I could not see it ever changing for the better. Despair and misery completely swallowed and immobilized me. I saw no way out. I thought this was it, this was the end.

Even so, I lived through the awful, endless night, and several months went by following that cold, lonely vigil. Eventually, I hustled up enough money to again buy myself a coat, a hat, and an umbrella. I even squirreled away enough to rent a tiny room from time to time. I was still miserable and merely existed from day to day, making no progress and having no future. I spent most of my time in the donut shop playing pinball, eating donuts, and drinking hot chocolate. The rest of my time was spent panhandling and trying to make a buck here or there. I felt like a zombie, and my life was going nowhere.

My start in life as a baby.

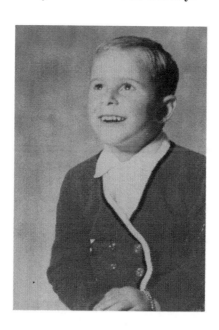

As a young boy. Good times ahead... or so I thought.

With my first family prior to break up.

With my second family prior to breakup. I was subsequently separated from my dad, brothers and sisters.

93

Growing up without my mom.

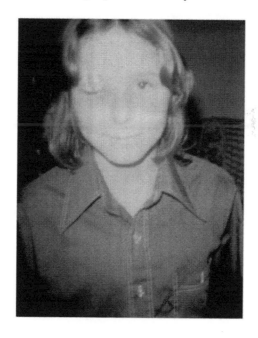

**The beginning of going from home to home in the foster care system.
Approx. age 12.**

Graduation from high school while in the Marine Corps.

Received metal from the Secretary for Heroism. 1980 Philippines

The United States Marine Corps.

In sniper school, learning the skills needed to become a top sniper.

Coming off a mission as a sniper back in 1982.

U S Marine Commandant award and meritorious mass citation from then Major General Grey.

From the Secretary of the Navy, a Metal for Heroism involving taking a live grenade away from a terrorist and trying to save lives while in the Philippines in 1981.

My wedding day. One of the greatest days of my life!

My wedding day. United States Marine sword ceremony!

Me with my wife and our four young children.

Our four children all grown up. So proud of each and every one of them.

Me, my wife, our four children, our daughter-in-law and our first grandchild.

Our four children. They grew up so fast and brought us so much joy.

My second son, whom I love so much.

My four children as teenagers.

With my wife, whom I love so very much, on Valentine's day.

With my daughter on Valentine's Day. She didn't have a boyfriend on this day so I made sure she wasn't left out!

My family celebrating the marriage of our oldest son, Scott, to his bride, Lynn.

Our 25th Anniversary

My wife and I on our 25th wedding anniversary. A great day for me!

Finally, John, my youngest son ties the knot and flees the nest (empty nest).

Groom and Bride, John and Chelsea Mulholland.

Vacation with my son, John, and our daughter-in-law, Chelsea.

A great day for my son and his wife as they build their dream home on their six acres.

My wife and I on a plane heading to Cancun, Mexico, for one of our clients.

My wife and I stopped in Seattle, Washington, where I, again, showed her where I grew up on the streets. Horse and buggy ride late one night.

Our three grandsons.

Me, with my son, Scott, and his three boys, Mason, Jackson and Hudson

My grandkids. Future Marines in training!

My grandsons going on a mission at night with their Papa, all in our Ghillie Suits.

Spiderman at work for US Building Consultants, Inc. Forensic Investigator for moisture engineering systems and controls.

My oldest son, Scott, just starting out in the family business.

Me repelling a multi-story commercial building. Who knew work could be so fun?

My growing company, Spiderman's Professional Services, Inc.

The Executive Staff at US Building Consultants, Inc.

My son, Scott, and me working on a job site together.

My son, Scott, and me at our corporate headquarters after making him the incoming President of the company when I stepped up to CEO.

Being Spiderman on the side of a building, 500 feet in the air.

Flying 35 MPH across the side of a high-rise building.

Spiderman on the side of a building with his oldest son, Scott Mulholland.

Spiderman on the side of a building with his youngest son, John Mulholland.

Teaching in Louisiana on the art of Sniper tactical operations and logistics.

Filming and training on tactical sniper techniques and marksmanship.

116

Out on the range keeping up with the marksmanship and training.

Out on the range keeping up with the marksmanship and training.

John Spence and I during one of his speaking seminars. Very provoking.

Spending eight days in Fiji with Tony Robbins at his private resort for his Business Mastery course. Great Time!

Giving University of Florida students a bible study in our home. Great people, students and athletes.

Baptizing one of the young ladies from our Bible Study.

Paintball with the university football team members.

My favorite quarterback and myself taking on the UF Gators in a head-to-head paintball game. We Won!

My mother and all her children reunited at a family reunion.

Another family reunion with my mother and all of her sons.

My role model, hero and brother. He inspired me to become a Marine.

Still my hero after all these years!

My Mom and her husband, George. This was such a happy time. I'm blessed to have them in my life.

My mother and I sharing a laugh and a hug during the celebration of my 50th birthday.

My reunion with Joe Schemnitzer

My reunion with Kathy Hoppenrath and her daughter, Debbie.

Meeting Joe

"There is no exercise better for the heart than reaching down and lifting people up."

—John Holmes

Chapter 18
Meeting Joe

I was at my very bottom when a man named Joe Schemnitzer came into my life and gave me a real leg up that helped me make it. If it hadn't been for this chance encounter with Joe, and for his genuine compassion and generosity, I would be dead today. No question about it.

While I was growing up, my home life was so far from the norm that most people find it hard to imagine, if not outright unbelievable. The fact is, I truly did not understand what a real, normal family was. I had no clear conception of how the members of a healthy, functional family interacted. Having never known any security, stability and predictable loving behavior, I was clueless, chronically hurting, and psychologically damaged by the absence of these critical qualities in my parents and our home life. Driven by my demons, and warped and wounded by my dysfunctional family, I had taken to the streets in the hopes of escaping my terror and pain at a very young age. Surviving in that dangerous, uncertain environment took all the skills I had in me and a great deal of luck. I did just about everything a person could do to survive – short of murder.

A family and personal life of drugs and abuse had left me scarred, vulnerable, and mistrustful. I lacked, because I'd never been taught, the basic life skills and social niceties. I could not fathom on my own how to simply get along with ordinary socially well-adjusted and functionally adept people. I didn't know what to say, or how to act or react in ordinary daily interactions with others. I distrusted everyone, did not believe anything anyone said, and I took it for granted everyone was out to get me or wanted to hurt me just for spite.

Then, unexpectedly and out of the blue, along came Joe, and he quite simply saved my life. He looked past all my rough edges and bad behavior and seemed to understand what had happened to me. Strangely, beneath my rough exterior, customary rudeness, and bad behavior, he saw something of worth in me, something worth saving. Fortunately, I was not too far-gone when Joe came into my world. Somewhere in the deep recesses of my mind, still a little hope remained. So, when Joe reached out and offered help, something in me said, "Take it – it may be your last chance!"

At the time, I was going on eighteen-years-old and had been living on the street for almost two years. Frankly, I wasn't going to live there much longer. Being killed was a very likely outcome the way I was going and the way I was living. In fact, between my first and second encounters with Joe, someone did shoot at me with the intent to kill me.

Fortunately for me, I grabbed his hand when Joe reached out to me, and my life was not just changed – it was saved. Initially, I was highly suspicious of him, didn't trust him at all, and from their scanty knowledge of him through very brief encounters, my street friends didn't trust him either. Everyone thought he must be after something, that he must have some plan to exploit me. Otherwise, why would he be interested in a bad kid like me?

Certainly, there were still major struggles ahead for me. Life did not change overnight. However, thanks to Joe, a first step had been taken. Joe had thrown me a lifeline, and because of that, I eventually became a productive member of society.

I met Joe one day while I was aimlessly walking around the streets. I had previously noticed a big brown 1973 Thunderbird and the big burly guy who was behind the wheel driving it slowly up and down the streets. I had seen the car lots of times before, but this time, the guy driving it was trying to seriously check me out.

Of course, from living on the streets, I was used to guys trying to pick me up, and I didn't like it at all. The way Joe was acting gave me the creeps and freaked me out.

He came around slowly again and again about six or seven times until he finally pulled over and tried to strike up a casual conversation with me. I didn't pay any attention to him, in fact I ignored him completely, and did not look right or left. I just stared straight ahead, not reacting or responding to his presence in any way, and I kept on walking. The next night, he showed up again at about the same time, between two and three in the morning. When I noticed him, I retreated to the alley, thinking that maybe he was an undercover police officer. He parked his car and walked up to a couple of other guys, acting friendly and interested in what they were doing.

He was big, about six-foot-six, and maybe two-hundred and thirty pounds. He was more than a little scary, but he had a nice face, a kind face. You might say he resembled a big teddy bear. As I stepped out of the alley, he saw me and introduced himself to me as Joe. I felt like he was trying to be just a little too nice to me. I smelled a fish.

"What's your angle," I asked him rudely.

"What angle?" he replied innocently. I sensed he was trying to play dumb and con me into something.

"You wouldn't be down here," I shot back with an ugly look on my face, "at three a.m. unless you wanted something."

He explained that he was a bar room bouncer, and he had just gotten off work.

"Are you a weirdo?" I asked him bluntly. If he were a pedophile, I certainly wanted to know.

"No, I'm not a weirdo!" he said a little too aggressively as if insulted and aggrieved. He looked hurt by my question and offended.

"Well, it doesn't make any sense for you to be standing on a street corner talking to us kids," I told him. "That is, unless you have a disgusting motive," I added.

"Well, big mouth," he was now talking loudly and directly to me, "do you enjoy living on the streets?"

"No!" I answered.

I stood there trying to size him up, figure him out and what he might be after, just wondering why he was wasting time talking to me and asking me all these questions.

"Do you want to go for a ride with me?" he asked me next.

"No way!" I said defiantly, repulsed by his offer and what it implied.

"OK, then would you be interested in getting some coffee and a donut?" he asked.

Hunger was my constant companion on the streets. The gnaw of hunger made my stomach ache most of the time and gave me terrible headaches. Yet it couldn't be helped. Usually, the money to get something to satisfy it was in short supply. I thought for a minute, and then I quickly agreed to go with him for a bite to eat. Even though I didn't know this guy, he had become oddly very interested in me when I told him I didn't want to be on the streets anymore. I was intimidated by him and a bit afraid of him because of his size, but I didn't let him know that. I kept my umbrella poised in a position to strike if need be and I was prepared to run away fast if I had to.

He parked his car, and we walked to the donut shop and got some donuts, coffee, and hot chocolate. After a while, I became convinced that he just simply wanted to know my story. He was easy to talk to, and as we sat there across the table from each other, I began to relax and let my guard down. As the minutes passed, I felt more and more comfortable being around him. Sitting there that night, we talked for a long time. He asked me questions with what appeared to be a real interest and concern for my welfare. After just a short time, I started to feel like he sincerely wanted to help me. At one point, he told me that I had a lot of potential, so for some reason, I got sarcastic with him and asked him if he wanted to be my Daddy.

"No," he said, "but maybe I could be your big brother."

When he said that, I almost burst into tears. I immediately thought of Brett. Wrenched with pain over all that I had lost, my brothers, sister and parents, I just fell apart. I jumped up from the table, pushed back my chair, said "Thanks, man," and ran out of the donut shop without another word. If Joe was trying to find my hot buttons, he had just scored big, let me tell you.

131

I ran fast and all the way to my apartment, and threw open the door. I found my ramshackle 'home' was even more disorderly than it normally was. Someone had gotten inside while I was away and totally ransacked the place. I kept a gun in my top drawer that a friend had recently given me as collateral on some money he had borrowed. Remembering that, I went straight to the drawer and opened it. Of course, it was gone, along with anything else I had of any value in that apartment.

Suddenly I heard a crack as a window pane shattered, and something hit the left side of the door at the top corner.

Oh, my God, I thought, someone has just shot at me! I felt something whiz by my head again, and I jumped to kill the light switch and then I hit the floor. I couldn't believe that someone was really shooting at me. My mind raced as I tried to figure out why someone would do this.

What had I done to make someone want to kill me? I tried to think who would do such a thing, but no names came to mind.

I stayed motionless on the floor in the dark until it occurred to me that whoever was doing the shooting might be coming up to my apartment after me. My third-floor apartment overlooked the alleyway between two buildings. Then it dawned on me that I was missing a gun, and someone had just shot at me. Maybe the same person who had robbed me was doing the shooting. As I cracked open my door, I looked down the hallway. Frozen in place, I was so scared I couldn't muster the courage to make a run for it.

Finally, my fear of being trapped in my apartment became greater than my fear of leaving, and I burst out the door and ran down the hallway. I raced around the corner to the apartment of an older black man who had befriended me. I stayed with him for a few hours but I never told him what had caused me to show up unannounced and uninvited at his place at such an early hour. As soon as it was daylight, I planned to get out of there.

It was only about six in the morning when the city began to come alive. I sneaked quietly into the lobby, trying to make myself invisible, and analyzing every face I saw, in an effort to identify someone in the crowd who could be carrying a gun and who would have tried to shoot me. I was alarmed when I realized that everybody in the room looked as if he could be that person. I was paranoid. Each person seemed to notice me and stare at me as if he wanted to bore his eyes right through my body. On feeling this sensation, I panicked and burst out of the main entrance of that old hotel building as fast as I could. Without pausing for even a second, I then raced down the street towards the park. Once there. I stayed around milling crowds of anonymous people in shops and restaurants until I worked my way back up to the apparent safety of Gunther's Donut House. I stayed there at Gunther's all afternoon that day, pretending to play at pinball, desperately hoping not to be discovered by whoever was trying to kill me.

Fear gripped me all day, nearly paralyzing me. I jerked my head around every time I heard the slightest sound or someone entered the donut shop. I was still convinced and scared out of my mind that at any minute someone was going to shoot at me again and perhaps kill me this time. Whatever I did, I couldn't seem to shake the feeling that someone was tracking me and trying to murder me.

Suddenly out of the corner of my eye, I noticed Joe's brown Thunderbird cruising slowly around in front of the Donut Shop. Without giving it any thought, I instinctively bolted out the door screaming, "Joe, Joe!" When I made it alongside his car, I frantically banged on his window, and he stopped to let me in.

"Hey, how are you doing?" he asked kindly, as I tried my best to calm down and catch my breath.

Completely terrified, I was pale as a ghost and visibly trembling from head to toe.

"Are you okay?" Joe asked again, carefully studying my face and demeanor. Joe knew what was what, obviously. No, he hadn't just ridden into town yesterday on a turnip truck, clueless about life on the street. He knew something was up and that I was in danger of some sort.

"Oh yeah, I'm fine!" I said again, trying to sound normal. "Why aren't you bouncing tonight?" I asked him.

"Tonight is my night off. Would you like to cruise around with me for a while?"

"Sure," I quickly agreed. With people trying to kill me, I could use a big bodyguard, but I tried not to sound too anxious.

"So, tell me some more about yourself," Joe asked me as we cruised around the neighborhood in his big car. So, I did. He wanted to know everything about me, and he was a good listener. I told him about where I had come from, why I had no home, and why I was on the streets at such an early age.

"You know, kid," Joe said, as he cast a glance my way, "you can get off the streets if you want to. I told my parents about you, and I'd like for you to meet them."

Wow, I thought, he wants me to meet his parents? What does he see in me? Someone seeing something good in me was a wholly new and unfamiliar behavior in the human race as I had known it up to that time. It was hard for me to get my head wrapped around it and believe it could be trusted to be what it claimed to be.

Over the next few months, Joe let me stay at his house. He was so giving and compassionate, characteristics that were totally foreign to me. Unfamiliar with it as honest, caring behavior and not some kind of lure or trap, I was, at first, only able to sneer at it and reject it, hoping to protect myself, not be conned, and to avoid being hurt, maybe even killed. That's what life had taught me to expect. From my own experience, I was unable to believe that real live people could behave like that and be sincere. You have to understand that my contact growing up with normal, reliable, decent people was almost non-existent, with the notable exception of our saintly neighbor Kathy Hoppenrath. Kathy Hoppenrath always took me in when my own mother, drunk out of her mind and violent, repeatedly over many years, kicked me out from the time I was two years old.

So it took me a long time to believe and trust in Joe. Yet he graciously introduced me to his warm accepting parents who lived with him at the time, and he gave me my own bedroom with a nice bed and other furniture. I was so damaged and fearful at that stage that I often became terrified at night when I was alone. I often begged him to let me sleep in his room next to his bed. Late at night, in tears, I'd frequently drag a

135

blanket with me into his room and sleep on the floor next to him. It was the only way I felt safe and could get some sleep. At night, I was always consumed with irrational fears and memories so painful that I'd weep at having them. But I felt safe in the presence of Joe. Eventually, I started calling him my "bodyguard," but mostly I thought of him as a wonderful big brother who really cared for me and who looked out for me all the time.

Joe took me with him as his little side-kick to many different places and introduced me to all his friends as his "little brother." In the morning, he dropped me off downtown, and I waited all day long until he could pick me up after leaving Transamerica, where he had his real job.

Sometimes his work took him out of town for a couple of days, and if he could, he took me with him. Every day that went by, he felt more and more like a real big brother to me. He gave me money sometimes and although it was tough, I quit hustling on the streets and started putting in applications for jobs. Since I was a high school dropout, with no prior employment or good work history, I still couldn't get a job.

Someone Was Looking for a Few Good Men

"Out of your deepest pain will come your greatest gifts; but this can only happen when you take control of the meaning."

—Tony Robbins

Chapter 19

Someone Was Looking for a Few Good Men

Finally, my long nightmare of living on the streets would seem to be over when Joe took me for a ride one day, and we ended up at the Seattle U.S. Army recruiting office. It was clear then that Joe had plans for me, reasonable plans, and he was not going to let me ignore the prospects and opportunities that I had.

But I took one look at the sign on the building and yelled "No way!" He turned to me with a puzzled expression on his face. Just to make sure he got the message, I yelled again, "No way! No way!"

"Okay, what's the problem?" he said patiently, turning to me as if he really wanted the truth about the issue I had with the Army. "So, why not, Scotty?"

"Joe! Listen to me," I said earnestly. "The only way I will go into the military is if I join the United States Marine Corps!"

"What? Why?" Joe asked.

I paused and thought a minute. My time in his company had created a bond between us that made me want to be honest with him about everything. As I did, I remembered fondly the pride and respect that I had for my oldest brother Tim when he enlisted in the Marine Corps. How proud of him I had been. How much I respected him for his enlistment and how quickly he had become my hero. No, no way was I going into the military unless I was going to follow in my revered older brother's footsteps.

Joe got it and approved of my sentiments. He urged me to follow my heart on this because if I didn't, I'd never be satisfied. So, with a lot of encouragement from my "big brother" Joe, I signed up for the Marines, and just two weeks later, I shipped out to boot camp in San Diego, California.

Wow. In an instant, I had changed course and made what was perhaps the most important decision I had ever made in my life, a decision which Joe had painstakingly and patiently convinced me was a real opportunity there for my taking. One I had never even considered. In no time, it proved to be a fateful decision that lifted me out of the depressing, self-defeating swamp of anger and despair that had immobilized me for so long and which had put me in a dumpster. With a timely assist from Joe, I had been given a push in the right direction that dramatically improved my circumstances. Yet it would take me years to fully understand and appreciate the huge significance of the Marine Corps' contribution to my life. It literally saved me from a wasteful life of poverty and petty crime. And it was a rescue made possible by the timely intervention of Joe Schemnitzer, a perfect stranger who took pity on me and tried to help me. Fine people like Joe can change someone's attitude and opinion of humanity.

Like a moth to a flame, though, I couldn't resist calling Mom and telling her that I had enlisted in the Marines and I was leaving. She met me at the airport and brought Gerald and Lisa with her to see me off. Mom was sober this time, and I cried. I had missed her so much. We had never talked the whole time I lived on the streets.

As we faced each other in the airport, I was now seventeen and a half years old, five-foot-five and only one-hundred and nine pounds. My hair hung way down my back, and I was dressed in a brown leather jacket, blue jeans and, of course, I carried my umbrella with the sharpened point.

It was so nice to see the three of them again. I had wanted to stay with Mom so badly, but I knew that if I did her drinking would soon have us at each other's throats. I never wanted to go back to a place like Boysville again. I knew I was about to become my own man and maybe put my horrifying childhood behind me. Nothing, however, could have ever prepared me for what I was about to experience.

I cried as I hugged Joe goodbye. I had become very close to him. I had never trusted anyone as I had learned to trust him. He had proven himself no less than absolutely trustworthy. He had indeed become the big brother I had needed so badly and just in time. The next bullet from a stray handgun in a dark alleyway may have ended it for me. It was so hard for me to leave him.

I felt as if I were losing a friend and now, as so many times in the past, another significant relationship was being stripped away from my life. It seemed as if everything good in my life was never meant to last because it always ended up ripped away from me. I had finally found a genuinely good person who believed in me, and here I was leaving him behind. To say I was reluctant to get on that plane is putting it mildly. Yet I had to admit that at least this time it was for an excellent reason.

Joe could see I was having second thoughts about leaving and again filled that "big brother" role to remind me that I had already signed up, and I had no choice but to show up at the Marine Corps base in California.

Well, I couldn't argue with that, so I hugged everyone goodbye one last time, and I walked up the ramp to board my plane and face my future.

Upon landing at the airport in San Diego, I resolutely boarded the OD-green bus sent to pick up the young recruits bound for the base. We soon arrived at the Marine Corps Recruit Depot in San Diego, California. To most, it was simply known as Boot Camp "Hollywood style." Because the base was in southern California and so close to Hollywood, we were called the "Hollywood Marines." Whoever came up with that nickname was either blind or stupid. There was nothing glamorous about us and surely nothing luxurious about our situation.

Not long after that, I got off the bus inside the base and a Marine staff sergeant wearing a hat that reminded me of "Smokey the Bear" instantly jumped in my face.

Less than an inch from my nose, he screamed at the top of his lungs, "You long-haired, slimy, sticky, maggot sissy, who do you think you are? Just look at you! You won't last a day in my Marine Corps!" he yelled like thunder.

I'm sure my face was pale and my eyes were as wide as saucers when he finished. This was not the kind welcome into the Marine Corps I had hoped for.

"Get your lousy carcass over there on them yellow footprints, lock your arms at your sides, and keep your eyeballs straight ahead!"

There was no mistaking those directions. He made all of us newcomers stand up straight and tall, and any offender quickly drew the wrath of not one, but several DIs (drill instructors), all wearing the same matching "Smokey the Bear" hats.

It took me less than five minutes to feel as if I had made a grave mistake. These people were mean and crazy, and most of them looked like body builders. I felt a huge knot developing in my stomach. Then, I made the mistake of trying to look at their faces to see if this was some game they were playing.

The drill instructor jumped right back in my face once more. Again, we were nose to nose and he was screaming so loud my ears were ringing.

"Get your eyes off me, maggot!" he yelled while his "Smokey the Bear" hat bumped the top of my head. Spit flew everywhere as he hollered, and I thought he was going to try to bite my nose right off my face!

"I did not give you permission to look at me, maggot!" he continued ranting.

Oh, my God, I thought, these guys think this is for real. They are dead serious. I need to get out of here! Fast!

Culture Shock, Becoming a Marine

I am a soldier, I fight where I'm told, and I win where I fight.

–George S. Patton

Chapter 20

Culture Shock, Becoming a Marine

Eleven weeks later, I left the MCRD in San Diego, California, but it was only after enduring every torment and physical and psychological trial the diabolical drill instructors and the USMC could throw at me.

In the end, I think I surprised everyone, myself included. It turned out that I performed very well in boot camp, well enough to graduate with a promotion to Private First Class, something only ten percent of graduates achieve. If life on the streets had taught me anything, it was how to survive. And believe me, there were plenty of times in boot camp when I felt like I might not. Everything about it was incredibly difficult.

However, I did survive. In fact, I did more than that. I excelled. I became physically fit, mentally tough, and had acquired a self-respect and confidence I never dreamed possible. Nothing could stop me now.

During my first year and a half as a Marine, I grew three inches and gained fifty-one pounds, most of it muscle. I started out running three miles in twenty-two minutes, forty seconds, and in just over a year, I ran that same three miles in sixteen minutes, forty-three seconds. I went through boot camp, infantry training school, and Camp Pendleton. In 1979, I shipped out to the Marine Corps Barracks in the Philippines for a fifteen-month tour.

There, they taught me "Kill and destroy" and "Rip their heads off and drink their blood." It was "Blood and Guts," and I loved every bit of it.

We were the finest fighting force on the face of the earth. We were mean, lean, and green. We were the United States Marines and we had a license to kill. The sense of pride and belonging is hard to describe. We were tough as nails and knew it, yet we were brothers, and our motto was Semper Fi (Always Faithful). We always had one another's back. I quickly fell in love with the concept of "Kill or be killed." I came from the streets, and I could relate.

I had completed the long journey from the lowest point in my life, barely alive on those mean streets, and was now, in what was really a very short time, a highly trained United States Marine who feared no man. They say what doesn't kill you, only makes you stronger. Perhaps all the abuse and sorrow of my childhood, losing my family the way I did, and my life's experience on the streets, had prepared me for the Marines.

However, all the anger, frustration, fear, and pain of my childhood had not simply disappeared miraculously, although I wish it had. Instead, it had now been turned into hate. I practiced hand-to-hand combat four hours every day, seeking to hurt or be hurt. On weekends, I partied, drinking like a fish, smoking pot, and taking drugs. I had developed a mindset of seeking revenge at all costs, but I was still somehow keeping it all together.

It was during this time during my assignment in the Philippines that I had the first unexpected test of my newly acquired status as a trained Marine. One otherwise ordinary day, while I was walking along Magsisi Drive in downtown Olongapo, I observed a Filipino man wrestling with two police officers in the street. I instinctively pushed through the big crowd to get a better look at what was going on.

As I did, the man wrestling with the police officers suddenly clasped his hands together and pulled the pin on a hand grenade. I looked on in

145

shocked disbelief. When the police officers saw this, they extended their arms and put their hands out in front them in a self-protective maneuver and to try to calm and caution the man to take it easy. But the man with the grenade would have none of it and instead screamed at them as he backed up right towards me, trying to put some distance between himself and the police officers. As he swung around to face the gathering crowd, it was evident that he had every intention of letting the grenade go, and I now stood only about six feet directly in front of him.

I knew if he dropped that grenade, I would be history, along with the innocent people behind and beside me. I was the closest one to him, so I did what I had been trained to do in a dangerous situation. I lunged toward him and grabbed his hand that held the grenade, locking my hands around his fingers so he couldn't drop and detonate it.

Then I pulled his hand up into the air and swept around behind him. From that position, I was able to force his arm back down around his back. I picked him up off the ground, as I kicked his feet out from under him and flipped him headfirst onto the concrete. That was enough to give me a chance to rip the grenade out of his hand and disarm him. The impact of his head against the concrete had knocked him out cold, and people screamed and ran in panic.

Two MP's had arrived just in time to see me plant this guy head first into the pavement. They didn't know what was going on and thought I was taking advantage of the guy, so one of the military police officers grabbed me by the shoulder and spun me around. As the hand grenade came into full view, the eyes of the MPs opened wide.

At that point, I finally became scared myself, because the pin had been pulled out of the grenade and the spoon was still on it. I was now afraid that all that movement might have moved the spoon or milked it, thereby igniting the fuse inside.

It would only take a few more seconds to find out.

The next ten or fifteen seconds ticked by very slowly and, I must tell you, chunks of my life flashed before my eyes. Those were by far the longest fifteen seconds of my life. When enough time had gone by, and I hadn't been blown into hamburger, I carefully handed the grenade over to the MP's and the Filipino police officers. They quickly taped up the spoon and concluded that luckily for everyone there, and especially for me, the grenade was a dud. I gladly left the scene, albeit a little weak in the knees.

Three weeks later, I was summoned to the colonel's office at headquarters. From a copy of the police reports, I found out a bit more about the person I helped capture. For my actions in disarming the man with the grenade, I was awarded the Secretary of the Navy Achievement Medal for heroism. I was also promoted to Lance Corporal and got another promotion when I moved from the job of Marine Sentry to the office of the Provost Marshal.

At the Provost Marshal's Office, I was assigned to the special operations branch, an elite group of Marines who provided special ops for the base security, including jungle patrols. We arrested local civilians suspected of various crimes and brought them in for questioning.

Some of the Marines in the squad used various means, some of which were considered unorthodox and questionable, to interrogate these prisoners. Here again, as on the streets of Seattle, I noticed that I seemed

147

to have a soft spot when it came to this type of coercive behavior. Some of the Marines I worked with didn't appear to have a conscience and didn't mind bending and breaking the rules in dealing with prisoners.

I abhorred this kind of behavior. It made me sick to know these men were cops. I always spoke out against it and even fought with other Marines I considered guilty of going too far to seek a conviction. Most of the time I won such scuffles since I had become very aggressive and very dangerous with my fighting techniques. During the year and a half that I remained in the Philippines, a master teacher in Olongapo taught me the technique of fighting open-handed, or 'tiger style' as they called it there. This gave me the unique fighting ability to hurt people who came against me when I appeared to be unarmed and defenseless. Even with this acquired skill, I still had a soft spot in my heart and didn't want to hurt others who were defenseless or see them set up dishonestly. On the other hand, I had no problem whatsoever hurting anyone who tried to attack me.

I still drank often and used drugs that were readily available in that part of the world. I had become bitter, and the chip on my shoulder became increasingly bigger. As I became aware of these changes going on within me, I grew disturbed. I didn't like what I was becoming; I had a lot of hate, bitterness, and frustration boiling up inside me. Such a disposition may have been advantageous to making me a killing machine, but it was wreaking havoc on me as a person and could potentially adversely affect my relationships with others.

When I finished my assignment in the Philippines, I found myself with orders stateside at Camp Lejeune, North Carolina.

Not long after my arrival at Lejeune, my company commander recognized my skill with an M-16 A1 rifle when I shot "expert" for the third time in a row. I recorded the high score of 238 out of a possible 250 on qualification day. One day, I shot an incredible 243 on the range and stunned all the other range officers. After hearing this, my company commander recommended me for sniper school, and I quickly shipped out.

Becoming a U.S. Marine Corps Sniper

"One shot. One kill. No exceptions."

—Tom Berenger, <u>Sniper</u>

Chapter 21

Becoming a U.S. Marine Corps Sniper

The Marines are polished military professionals, highly skilled in the art of combat and killing. They have more than 240 years of history backing up their nickname "Devil Dogs." That was the name given to them by the Germans in France during World War I. The intense training, discipline, and the motto "Semper Fi" (Always Faithful), breeds something special in the spirit of each Marine that makes them the finest fighting force on Earth. The Marines are the first to fight because the President can send them to hotspots anywhere in the world before Congress needs to get involved in a declaration of war. Wherever and whenever they are needed, they are always ready to respond by land, sea, or air.

My enrollment in sniper school was an experience I'll never forget.

Fascinated by the techniques taught by the instructors, I quickly learned the school possessed one of the highest dropout rates of any military training curriculum. It was rated the most difficult training school to complete in all the Marine Corps. For ninety days, sixteen to twenty hours a day, seven days a week, a man's vision, desire, and commitment were severely challenged – mentally, physically, and psychologically. Endurance, along with a lot of guts, gall, and tenacity, were only part of the course.

Memorization, knowledge, stealth and patience were also vital in passing the course. I began the class with almost fifty of the top handpicked Marines selected for the training, but in the end, only fourteen of us graduated from the school.

What caused such a dropout rate and kept a majority of my class from finishing? It was the commitment to excellence required to finish. I soon found out that to become one of the top-trained snipers in the world, some abilities just had to be God-given. It was obvious that some special talents could neither be developed nor taught. Either people arrived with them, or they flunked out.

Part of the difficulty in the training was that there were never any days off. Every day for three months, sometimes twenty hours a day, the training tested our commitment. Getting up every day at four-thirty in the morning to run five miles in full camouflage uniform would test any man's commitment. I constantly asked myself, "Do I really want to be a sniper? Is it really worth this?"

Some Marines who were heavier than I was fell back or pulled off to the side. Sniper instructors fell back as well and kicked the stragglers back into a run. The verbal abuse and physical punishment meted out by instructors to those who did not keep up with the group seemed to pull energy from inside me that I never realized I had. While the rest of the class took showers and ate breakfast, the ones who fell out or didn't finish spent hours doing push-ups, sit-ups, or ran in place, missing their showers and breakfasts.

I decided very early on that I wasn't going to fall back in the early morning runs and become a target for such attacks.

Apart from the physical challenges, the amount of time we devoted in the classroom to memorization of opposing forces' infantry units was every bit as grueling. Snipers had to be able to pick out an officer in uniform of any potential opposing military unit that was not an ally of U.S. forces. One of our daily training exercises called Kim's games involved the placement of fifty objects on a table with a towel covering them. When the towel was removed, sniper students had only one minute to study the objects and memorize them, followed by two minutes to remember the objects and write them down.

At first, I could only remember about 14 to 18 of those fifty objects, but after three months of training, my recall had become so refined that I could remember a large majority of them after only twenty seconds of viewing them. This exercise was vital in teaching us to focus on details, memorize terrain features, and quickly take notes as we gathered information as a scout-sniper team.

Part of our mission was to train for reconnaissance or scouting. At other times, we had to "take out" an opposing key military figure or target. Our shooting skills had to be virtually perfect. One shot had to equal one kill, period. Stalking perfected stealth to the target. This was where Marine snipers got their nickname "The battlefield boogeymen."

You would never see or hear a sniper, but he would always see you. During stalking, or what we called "snooping and pooping," we built ourselves a specialized uniform called a "ghillie suit."

The word ghillie was an old Scottish term for a particular kind of game warden. Ghillies were tasked with protecting the game on the land of their Scottish Lord. From time to time, the ghillies mingled with the game by hiding in the grass and lying perfectly still, and then they surprised and attacked any poachers or natural predators to ward them off.

We spent late night hours constructing our ghillie suits piece by piece, gluing burlap strips onto our camouflage uniforms. We cut up the sturdy material of sea bags and stuck them to the front of our ghillie suits to give us extra padding to make crawling more comfortable. The entire uniform was covered in the burlap strips that had been glued and sewn into it.

Once the finished suit was on, a sniper could drop down in grass or the woods, and someone could step on him before detecting him. The ghillie suit made the shooter virtually invisible by breaking up any typical distinguishing physical features. Once the sniper was completely camouflaged, he took his M 40A1 Remington 700 308-caliber rifle and stalked his target.

In one type of training exercise, we were dropped from a large military truck approximately two-thousand yards away from a target area. We then approached it by crawling on the ground. Skilled officers trained in sniper detection were stationed on the truck and equipped with 7x50 binoculars watching a field approximately nine-hundred feet wide and two-thousand feet long trying to detect us. The shooter's task was to get within one-hundred feet of the truck and fire twice at the officers, while undetected.

As an additional neutral observer, a Marine with a field radio walked, under the command of the officers in the truck, to any location on the field where they thought they had spotted movement and tried to find us. If we could get within one-hundred feet of the vehicle and successfully shoot twice still undetected with all eyes on us, the neutral Marine on the ground would hear the shots, locate us, and come within five feet of us. If still undetected from the truck, he would move in and touch our head with his hand. If the watching officers still could not see the sniper at one-hundred feet away with 7x50 binoculars, the sniper would successfully pass one stalk.

Each Marine had to pass nine out of the twelve stalks to qualify as a sniper. Obviously, this was where most of the class failed. It was an incredibly difficult task, especially since we were given only four hours to complete the objective.

The words 'invisible' and 'undetectable' were burned into our way of thinking. What they asked us to do was almost impossible, but they had chosen top Marines who understood cover and concealment techniques, along with an acute sense of their own movements and motion.

During those three months of training, we learned many things. Along with learning how to become invisible and undetectable, we also developed the marksmanship skills to hit an eight-inch wide helium balloon, blowing in the wind, with one shot, from six-hundred meters away. We also had to do things like find a shell casing hidden in the woods two-hundred meters away with our binoculars in only fifteen minutes. Finally, we had to find our way back to camp after being dropped off in the darkness of night at a distance of three days' travel away.

Although the school pushed me to my absolute limits, I excelled with a passion for the unique and sophisticated training that enhanced my abilities and was proud to be honored with that title and achievement of becoming a member of one of the top sniper teams in the world. Since the United States Marine sniper school was considered "the best of the best," I was fortunate to graduate as the top sniper/marksman shooter and fourth overall in my class. I later became a Scout Sniper Instructor and taught those same skills to others in various battalions and special operations teams for the next eighteen months.

Training in Special Operations

"Let your plans be dark and impenetrable as night, and when you move, fall like a thunderbolt."

—Sun Tzu, The Art of War

Chapter 22
Training in Special Operations

I was next transferred to Headquarters & Service Company, Third Battalion, Second Marine Division, where I became a member of an STA Team in a Surveillance Target Acquisition Platoon. We received some of the best training in the military, and so were deployed on a regular basis.

During this time, I was sent to Korea for three months to attend mountain warfare school. There we learned counter-guerrilla operations and terrorist tactics. Performing specialized assaults out of helicopters while in Japan fascinated me, since getting in and out of enemy lines was one of my "specialties." On one occasion, we were involved in an enormous simulated war game. During that phase of training, a particular specialty of mine really became apparent.

Thousands of Marines took part in this three-day event, and it was as close as you could get to the real deal. We simulated live attacks and ambushes and took prisoners. Everything was made as real as humanly possible, except for the ordinance and ammunition, of course. Case history decided who lived or died, based on the scenario involved. The judges wore white armbands; our team of Marines wore red, and the enemy Marines wore blue. Our company commander was confident we would prevail and informed us that we would, "Not lose this simulation." We were not going to embarrass his command.

He called on his special ops teams to conduct search and destroy missions, but at the same time, he also wanted to get as much intelligence as he could. He selected a scout and me to pinpoint pockets of resistance.

At night, we used 'nod' and 'Starlight scopes' that, when looking through them, lit up the night as if it were day. Special sensors and radars pinpointed tracked vehicles and large movements by the "enemy forces."

We plotted positions, called in air strikes, and sent in recon teams to hit the enemy's weak flanks. Our information was vital and pushed the war games dramatically in our favor. Our STA team was very sophisticated, and we had the trained personnel and equipment to protect our battalion from sneak attacks and to strike at our unsuspecting enemy. On the third or fourth night of the operation, we received intelligence indicating that our enemy's headquarters were temporarily set up on our main front. However, lines of Marines and machine gun bunkers protected us against a frontal attack.

At sundown, I alerted my captain that I was going in. At approximately nineteen-hundred hours, or 7 p.m. that night, my scout and I disappeared just past our front supporting lines. Decked out in our ghillie suits, with night goggles and a starlight scope, we headed for the enemy lines.

Over the course of the next four hours, I managed to stalk undetected right into the midst of their base camp. We slipped in between sentries and a full group of Marines who were talking among themselves. About midnight, my scout stayed behind as I crept onward, drawing from everything I had learned in becoming a sniper. Marines walked all around me, and I shook and trembled unseen as the adrenaline raced through my body.

By 1:00 a.m., everything had become quiet, and every little noise or breaking of a twig was magnified. I slowly and methodically crawled

159

through the compound, using shadows and staying away from any points of possible foot traffic. To my complete surprise, I noticed a tent with the company commander's flag on it. I also saw high-quality screened-in bug netting, along with an excellent, non-electric coffee pot and mugs, and some comfortable foldout chairs. This was much too extravagant for an ordinary Marine. I had indeed discovered the commanding officer's tent.

Although it was guarded by about a fifty-foot perimeter, I got within the circle of sentries protecting it, and soon found myself lying on the ground right next to the CO's tent. I couldn't believe my luck! I had "snooped and pooped" right up to the highest-ranking enemy officer on the battlefield without being detected.

I knew that if this were a real combat situation, I would pull his tent peg up, crawl into his tent, and quietly slice his throat.

Since this was only a simulated war game, instead, I only needed to simulate his death without detection. I gently and carefully worked up one tent peg that held down a corner of his tent, followed by a second tent peg, and then I worked my way inside. With my pupils fully dilated, since I hadn't looked at any light for at least several hours, I had what we called "cat eyes;" a condition that allowed me to see clearly in almost total darkness.

I could see the cot with the captain sleeping on it, a table with a large map, and various supplies. I noticed his camouflaged uniform jacket, with two of the most beautiful silver captain's bars I had ever seen, pinned correctly to the lapel. With his rank insignias staring me in the face, I gently moved over to his uniform, pulled both of his captain's bars off, and slipped them into my pocket.

By now, my heart was pounding so hard I could feel it on the ground, as I lay flat on my stomach. Sweat poured from my forehead, and my body shook with both excitement and fear of detection. My scout and I are about to take out the greatest enemy element in this war game, I thought. However, I also knew that my slow movements and stealthy maneuvers had taken most of the night, and the darkness would soon slip away. I had less than three hours to get back out of the enemy camp, through hundreds of Marines, and remain undetected before sunrise. It seemed impossible.

There was no way to move that fast without detection because of the cracking of a small twig or movement in the ten to twelve-inch underbrush. I panicked inside at the thought of being caught and embarrassing my company commander.

I could not bear the thought of graduating as one of the top snipers, only to be caught on my first simulated mission. Something in me screamed, "NO, NO, NO!"

I had failed at so much in life, and I didn't want to be a failure here. Combined with my aching desire for someone to be proud of me, you could say I was highly motivated to succeed. I simply had to get those captain's bars back to my battalion and show it to a referee of the war game, so that I could get credit for the kill.

I quickly but silently moved out of the captain's tent. I gently pushed away the tent flap, when I heard the captain move in his cot. I froze in fear. My back and head were facing away from him. I thought he had heard me and had awakened.

If he catches me, I thought, he'll mock the skill and reputation of the sniper, the most feared special ops on the battlefield.

My whole body trembled with fear, yet I was frozen motionless. I felt that the captain had rolled over and was just staring at me. Five more minutes went by as I dared to barely breathe. As the minutes passed without a sound, I knew that if he had seen or detected me, he would have already responded. Slowly, I turned my head and looked back into the darkness of the tent. I couldn't see his eyes, only the dark silhouette of his body resting on that cot. After watching him for a while, I determined that he was still fast asleep. It took another thirty minutes for me to get out and reset his tent pegs.

I knew I was in trouble. The sun was going to come up in only a couple of hours, and I would lose the protective cover of the night.

To my surprise, by that time several sentries had gathered together outside the tent, drinking coffee and talking among themselves, trying to keep from falling asleep while they were on post. From time to time, this created significant gaps in the middle and upper front lines. Because of this, I was able to move quickly from behind the enemy lines and reach our camp before sunrise.

Once there, I immediately notified my lieutenant of our success. He quickly woke our captain to inform him that his #1 scout-sniper team had just taken out the enemy's company commander. His eyes lit up when I pulled out the rank insignia of his fellow officer, who was acting as his war game enemy. Without his enemy in the game and the strategic guidance and leadership he could provide, the effectiveness of his troops would be reduced, and their morale would suffer.

We received a strong handshake and a tremendous "Job well done!" Impressing the company commander was not an easy thing to do, but it was evident that my scout and I had proved our ability and the need for our special operations teams to work within his battalion. The judge quickly recorded the incident and escorted him in a Jeep to the enemy's base camp.

Still clad in my sniper ghillie suit and flanked by my captain and lieutenant, we walked with the judge into the camp of the "enemy." They yelled and taunted us, as our red armbands stood out among the hundreds of blue ones. Although this was just a simulated war game, we were all excited and into the psychological mindset of the real thing.

"Enemy sniper! Incoming enemy sniper! Incoming!" yelled the perimeter sentries.

As they taunted and mocked us, I was shocked at the disrespect the enemy showed to my officers in charge. It wasn't customary to approach the enemy during war games, so the judge wearing the white armband pushed us through the yelling simulated enemy. My captain took the rank insignia I had delivered to him and handed them back to me. He smiled as we approached the "enemy" captain, who was now standing outside his tent guarded by ten of his Marines. Over one-hundred weapons loaded with blank rounds were pointed at us.

As we met the other captain, I noticed that his uniform jacket had two small holes on each side of his lapel, right where his captain bars used to be.

The judge walked up to him and looked at the officer, then looked back at me. I tried not to smile. It took everything in me not to explode with pride at what I had accomplished, something many would consider impossible.

I looked at the enemy captain straight in the eye and firmly said, "You're dead, sir!"

Everything stopped – silence reigned. You could have heard a pin drop. No one said a word for several seconds. The enemy officer appeared puzzled and stared at the judge in disbelief, looking for an explanation. I waited as long as I could, savoring the moment, before showing my proof. Then I stuck out my hand and opened my tight-fisted palm, revealing the two shiny captain's bars.

"You're dead, sir!" I said loudly and firmly again, with a voice full of pride and accomplishment. The officer, in disbelief, quickly pulled his collar down feeling for his rank insignia, which, of course, were gone. Apparently, when he had put his uniform jacket on in the early morning, he had not even realized he had been stripped of his rank. That was all the proof the judge needed, and he ordered the officer off the field of play.

My ranking officers quickly turned and walked away, and I followed. I could hear the enemy captain exploding in an angry tirade at the men who had been charged with guarding him during the night. The yelling continued as we drove out of the base camp.

The Accident That Changed My Life

"Faith is taking the first step, even when you don't see the whole staircase."

—Martin Luther King, Jr.

Chapter 23
The Accident That Changed My Life

I was sent on many more missions and had many amazing experiences as a sniper over the next couple of years, but none of them as memorable as that day when I held those two captain's bars in my hand.

No matter what my life had been like and how defeated I had felt while I lived on the streets, nor how much of a failure I had been in my adolescence, I excelled in everything in my career as a Marine. No matter what I was asked or required to do, I performed well. As a Marine, I soon realized that the key to achievement and success in anything was all about mindset. The Marines taught me to be mentally tough, to rely on myself, and to never stop until my mission was completed.

Self-reliance, determination, persistence: they were invaluable character qualities that equip you for all of life's challenges. I have the Marine Corps to thank for teaching them to me and demonstrating unforgettably how to use them in my daily life.

Nevertheless, even with my successes at that stage, my life still felt hollow and incomplete. I still had no real family to spend loving time with, and the pain of my childhood kept forcing itself into the foreground of my thoughts, regardless of how hard I tried to suppress it. Every time I thought of my family at night, the tears welled up. Many nights I actually did cry myself to sleep because I missed everyone so much. I continued to use drugs and alcohol as a way of dealing with the silent pain I lived with every day and every night. I pushed myself in martial arts, purposely sparring with those who held the rank of 'black belt' and who were much better than I was, trying to learn from them and improve my skills. The fact that they drew blood or could possibly break one of my bones did not deter me.

For whatever psychological reason, I somehow felt that I deserved to be beaten up, or punished for something. I could not be successful for a long period of time without somehow destroying my success. I was used to nothing but being hurt and beaten up physically and mentally for everything I did.

Now that I was successful as a Marine and excelled in everything I tried to do, everyone suddenly respected me and never really had anything negative to say to me. My superiors and my peers both liked and respected me. This was an entirely new concept for me, and I just wasn't used to it. Instead, I beat myself up mentally, and I suppose, through martial arts, physically, thinking I didn't deserve anything good.

No matter what I accomplished as a Marine, that success was overshadowed by the pain, guilt, and loneliness of my childhood. I was twenty years old now, but I still felt like a twelve-year-old boy wanting his Mom and Dad. I felt like damaged goods.

Looking back now, this dysfunctional thinking drove me to rely on the drugs, alcohol, and martial arts. It was like I had a death wish and I was just waiting for someone to take me out of my loneliness and pain. I poured my life into the Marine Corps; it became my new family. I loved what it stood for and the prestige it gave me. However, it did little to improve my emotional state or my ability to cope with the psychological pain of my past.

Drugs and alcohol were my temporary solution to this problem. I tried to quit many times and even sought professional help, but nothing seemed to work.

Meanwhile, despite my issues, my career accelerated. I was promoted to Corporal and then was recommended for meritorious promotion to Sergeant. I received two meritorious service awards and was chosen for special schools and privileges. Although on the outside I was mean, lean, and green, with an extra strong dose of motivation and commitment, on the inside, my life was falling apart. Something was missing, and no one seemed to have the answer for me. I kept searching for something, but I had no idea what I was looking for.

During this anguished, uncertain time in my life, another Marine, a friend of mine, and I took a drive from North Carolina where I was stationed at Camp Lejeune to Washington, D.C. to get away for the weekend. We were just outside of the city when my life once again changed forever.

A semi tractor-trailer had just slowly passed us and pulled a few car-lengths ahead of us. Suddenly, we noticed smoke coming from his tires. The driver had locked up his brakes at 65 MPH, and the cab of the truck had instantly jerked back around toward us. We heard the squeal of the tires on the pavement and the sound of the truck jack-knifing almost right on top of us. My friend, who was driving, took evasive action, so we were not crushed by the massive trailer. Instead, we skidded off the highway and came to a stop on the side of the road, just barely missing a nearby house.

I was in a fog of shock, but at least we were miraculously both alive and unhurt. As my vision cleared and I regained my senses, I looked up and saw that the tractor-trailer had fully jackknifed and skidded out of control almost entirely off the highway. Another car had hit it, bounced off the 18-wheeler, and came to rest off of the highway not far from us in a mangled, smoking, twisted mess of metal. Confident that my friend was all right, I jumped out of our car and ran over to the badly wrecked car to see if I could help.

What I found and what happened next would change me forever. When I got to the other car, I discovered an elderly woman slumped and unconscious in the driver's seat. She had sustained major injuries. I had to get her out of the car. It was clear her injuries were life-threatening. Every second counted. So I reached in and gently lifted her out of the seat, easing both of our bodies onto the grass a short but safe distance away, resting her fragile bleeding head in my lap. The elderly woman took just a few more short breaths of air, then let out a long gasp. As she did, I felt the air and the life leave her body. She had died in my arms as I looked on, helpless to save her.

As the older lady expired in my arms, yes, at that exact moment, I heard a loud voice, as loud and terrifying as deafening thunder, say unmistakably, "That is your last chance!"

I held this poor old lady in my arms whose soul had only just fled, but it was the thunderous voice that had shaken me to my core.

Hearing a voice from the sky, having the dead lady in my arms, with the wreckage of the eighteen-wheeler and cars scattered all over the highway, I was very sobered at the thought that we had barely escaped sudden death. My head hurt and my mind was wracked with shock as the trauma slowly registered in my consciousness.

That's when the full weight of the catastrophe and our narrow escape from the jaws of death finally hit me. I was convinced. It was clear. The voice I had heard was none other than the voice of God. He had spoken directly and personally to me. Me. Although I had of course known about God all my life, I had also seen a lot of "religion" and religiosity that had repelled me and completely turned me off to the concept of serving Him. As a result, I was not the religious or church-going type.

Ironically perhaps, only two weeks before this awful accident, two Christians had approached me out of the blue and passionately tried to "witness" to me about Christ. They were ardent true believers, real soldiers of the faith. No surprise then that we ended up having a heated, argumentative discussion.

"Where is God?" I rudely asked, challenging their smug certainty in my ignorant pride and arrogance. "If God is real, where is He? Why do bad things happen to millions of good people if God is real, merciful, and loves us as you claim? If God is real, why doesn't He show Himself to us and prove once and for all that He is really real?" Then, thinking back to my abusive childhood, the remembered pain and anger boiled out of me, and I taunted them.

"Show me your God! Where is He?" I shouted at them.

Intimidated and insulted, the two men retreated from my rude blasphemy and gave up trying to witness to me. I was overwrought and belligerent. Frightened by my bizarre behavior, they ran away from someone whom I am sure they considered an obvious maniac and maybe a dangerous sociopath.

Yet now, after having heard God's voice at the site of the fatal accident, the reality of human mortality had been clearly demonstrated to me. I was forced by my own senses to admit that there might indeed be a God or Supreme Force, spiritual and powerful, capable of intervening in human lives, that can and will communicate with us. When the Voice said, "That's your last chance," I knew exactly Who was speaking to me and what the words meant. It was instant, intuitive and inarguable. Yes, you could say that I got the message.

God had become active and apparent in my life. Those two faith-filled Christians, along with some similarly inspired fellow Marines only a few weeks before, had tried to bring me to Christ, to get me to go to church and to accept God into my life. Yet their pleas and protestations fell on deaf ears, for in my view, Christianity was nothing more than a cult of gullible hypocrites. I looked at it as nothing more than a crutch for the weak.

At that time, I did not realize that every person had to deal with the spirit within himself, his own soul, and I had no real interest in that. I was angry about how life had treated me growing up and had forced me to live on the streets, so I was immune to the message of those compassionate missionaries who had tried to reach me. They were good people who had recognized my pain and confusion, and I had rejected them. I had taunted and insulted the men sent by God to witness to me. I had sneered and refused to go to church when my friends pleaded with me.

It was my last chance to accept the Lord into my life as my savior. I would have no peace or real comfort until I did.

For months after the accident, I couldn't shake the thought of that sweet elderly woman dying in my arms or the blaring spectral Voice I heard at the time, the Voice that still echoed in my ears and thoughts, warning me over and over again that I had run out of time and options.

I was scared to death by this ultimatum. I knew I needed redemptive spiritual help, I knew that I desperately needed "Amazing Grace." But for some reason, I hesitated. I just could not make the leap of faith that this choice required. I could not fully accept that this was the remedy to what was wrong with me, that it was the healing cure for the gaping wounds in my heart and soul that ached all the time and made me so unhappy.

Besides, I thought that being a Christian would probably mean that I could no longer drink, smoke, or party on weekends. Those were unthinkable deprivations for me. How would I be able to tolerate the daily anxiety, fear and torment of my excruciating memories without booze and drugs? How? Impossible. I was sure my life would be insupportable without them.

There was no way that I was going to live such a hypocritical life. I was not going to go to church to be an angel on Sunday, only to live like the devil the rest of the week. If I were going to be a Christian, I wanted to be a real one.

After the accident, I tried to pray in my own way, and occasionally I read the Bible. I felt an inner pressure to do something, and I kept hearing that loud Voice in my mind. The message was very sobering. But I was torn between two worlds, with mountains of emotional baggage in

172

between. Yes, something was happening in my life. I felt a spiritual stirring deep within me, I heard soft whispers of solace. I listened, I dreamed, I thought. I found myself trying to talk to the Voice, but the mental picture projected on the screen of my mind depicting God as my Father caused a flood of conflicting emotions to surface.

I discovered that I didn't know how to have a true and deep relationship with God. I didn't even know who or what God was or how to approach Him. How could I love God when I did not even love myself? How could I possibly believe God would forgive me when I could not forgive myself? I'd had no parental training or guidance or exposure to church or spiritual tradition of any kind. I knew no prayers nor how to pray on my own. I only knew small parts of the Bible, and the Gospels only by hearsay and isolated reading.

What I did know, what I sensed deep within me, was that in spite of the absence of spiritual training in my background and lack of spiritual resources, God still somehow knew all about me. He knew how bad I felt all the time. He knew that I desperately needed relief from the pain I had to fight just to make it through the day and night. He knew how it distracted and handicapped me, and blocked me from establishing loving, caring relationships with others. I knew in my bones that He wanted to help me. I knew He would have to know the pain and confusion I struggled with every minute of every day.

After the accident, in a matter of a few weeks, it became perfectly clear to me that God was close by and watching every move I made. He heard every word I spoke and He cared for me. Yet none of that knowledge and intuition of God made Him attractive to me or made me want to go running into His arms for protection and help as if He were my Father.

"That's your last chance." Every day I lived with the unnerving Voice echoing in my head. I developed a kind of paranoia because of it. I became convinced that if I didn't turn my life around and become some saintly Christian within a certain period of time, then 'POW!' I would be dead.

I felt a small tug on my heart to go to church, but I was turned off by the multitudes of so-called good people claiming to be Christians, who were flagrantly not acting like Christians at all.

Despite all my straining and efforts to sort this muddle out and make the right decision, I kept hitting a wall.

The Book Was Right, Not the Preacher

"The Lord is nigh unto them that are of a broken heart; and saveth such as be of a contrite spirit."

-Psalm 34:18(KJV)

Chapter 24

The Book Was Right, Not the Preacher

Several weeks after the accident, I dipped my toe in the water of faith by attending a Bible study. I began to read the Bible on a regular basis, but as before, I didn't get much out of it because I didn't understand it. I started going to church, and when I asked what I should do to help the process along and to feel closer to God, several preachers told me to say a prayer, and that I would be saved.

This really upset me, since I could see that it was nonsense. Saying a few words to accept the Lord as my personal Savior, while I still lived in bondage to a lifestyle of drugs, alcohol, cigarettes, and partying just didn't seem like it was enough. I lived most of that lifestyle just to cover and survive my pain.

I really felt that no matter how much faith I might have, merely saying a few automatic, pre-fab words to the Lord was not going to completely deliver me. Besides, after carefully searching the Bible, I soon found that "Accepting the Lord as my personal Savior," wasn't even an accurate quotation of scripture.

That phrase was not consistent with the verses I read in John 3: 3-5, which said, "Except a man be born again of water and of the Spirit, he cannot enter the kingdom of God."

Jesus never said anything about accepting him as a personal Savior. It wasn't like I would wake up one day and accept Him. The real key was, did God accept me. I was the one who was lost, not God! However, He did say that we needed water and Spirit. Everyone seemed to have his or her own opinions and interpretations of what this meant, a fact which confused me even more. I didn't know who to believe, or what to believe. I had no idea where to turn. I only felt more alone, and I became even more depressed than ever.

Once again, I resorted to drugs and alcohol, but just as before, it was nothing more than a cheap, temporary fix. In my search for the truth, I went to several churches, Bible studies, and prayer meetings. I tried within myself to live righteously, and I even tried to cut out some of my bad language. However, I just couldn't seem to get deliverance.

I was bound up, miserable, and hurting inside. Everything I saw and heard appeared to be only the fake outward display of being a Christian and "being saved." It was all superficial and only skin deep.

It was not even clear to me exactly what I was being saved from. What exactly was salvation? That was my big question.

And how could these so called Christian people say they were going to heaven but still live their lives like devils? I finally realized that I did not want religion; I wanted Jesus Christ instead. To change my life, I began to diligently search the scriptures. Everyone had their own opinion, including myself, and I did not trust others' opinions, let alone my own understanding of the Bible or personal belief system.

I did, however, believe that the Bible contained the truth and I knew it had to be right. I also read in Revelation that the Apostles' names were written in the foundations of gold and that Jesus said He lost none of them except Judas. If Peter had the keys to heaven, it became very simple to me that if I would only do what they did, I could not be lost. If what the

Apostles did and preached was correct, I reasoned that all I had to do was follow their examples to be saved.

I spent about a month studying the New Testament, and in Acts, I read how the disciples were saved. I knew what they preached, and I realized I did not have what they had, nor did I believe what they believed. I looked up every description in the Bible of how the Apostles were saved, and what they told others to do to be saved. I could not find any verse of scripture that said "[You must] accept Jesus as your personal Savior," nor could I find a verse saying that I should be baptized according to Holy Trinity, as some people were telling me.

In the end, I took the examples I found in the book of Acts, and I repented of my sins to God on my own.

Shortly after that, I went to church again and during the service, we came to the part of the service in which the church leaders laid their hands on me. When they did, instantly my life changed forever. The moment they put their hands on my shoulders, my legs simply gave out, and I fell to the floor. I was stunned. Even stranger than that was what happened afterward. For as I lay there on the floor incapacitated for more than two hours, I was speaking in another language, one that I did not understand at all. The event was unlike anything I had ever witnessed or experienced.

When I could finally get back on my feet, I was then baptized in the Name of Jesus, and I was a new man. Subsequently, for more than thirty-five years after that, I have never again touched alcohol, drugs, or attempted suicide. For me, it was a watershed moment. It's clear to me today that getting the spiritual side of my life in order counts as the major victory of my life.

Yet the focus of this book is not about finding God and being saved. I totally believe people can excel in life without being spiritually connected with God, just as I excelled and developed lifelong friends in the Marines before I was saved. Nevertheless, I do feel I am living proof that you can go so much further if you get things right with your Creator; and I know, without any doubt whatsoever, that my faith is a critical force and an integral part of my success and my life story.

Hey, I may be crazy, but I'm not stupid. I have decided that for me, I'm not going through all the hell I've endured just to in the end up in a burning hell with all the wicked and disobedient souls. Besides, the retirement plan is out of this world!

Finding My Soul Mate

Who can find a virtuous woman? For her price is far above rubies.

Proverbs 31:10 (KJV)

Chapter 25

Finding My Soul Mate

I was a new man after finding Jesus. Gifts and blessings started pouring into my life from many directions. I was amazed.

Of all the amazing events granted to me after my faith conversion and commitment, though, none was more welcome or enduring than discovering my darling Tina, my permanent life partner and soulmate, in the same humble North Carolina church where I found Jesus. God had answered my most heartfelt prayer and relieved me of the terrible pain of loveless isolation and the searing anguish of loneliness.

Tina and her family had been loyal members of the congregation for many years. The church was a warm, welcoming family church in the truest sense. Yes, a family church in every way.

Congregants reached out to and supported one another in good times and bad. The church congregation itself was one big indissoluble family, sanctified and joined together in the Name of Jesus.

Yet, for Tina and me, unlike the fairy tales and the romance novels, it was not "love at first sight." Not at all, though she was obviously a beautiful and virtuous young woman. But I was not attending church services to pick up women. I was there, I hoped, to be noticed and "picked up" by God!

Eventually, however, I observed her several times in church praying, and I was struck by her deep love and devotion for the Lord. She set an impressive example for me of a faith wholly embraced, a faith totally integrated into a person's thoughts, dreams, and daily life.

The truth is, before I loved her, I revered her as a spiritual role model for what I hoped my behavior would become under the transformative power of God's saving grace. Well, as events unfolded, my judgment was validated many times over. Time proved that I could not have picked a better spiritual role model or lifelong partner and companion.

Months and seasons passed. I looked forward to Sundays more and more. I became acquainted with and endeared myself to Tina's warm and loving family. We spent more and more time together as a family ourselves, a miraculously healing and restorative process for me, a contented and secure state previously unimaginable to me after what I had lived through as a child. It was and continues to be unto this very day what saved my life and what has sustained me over the years through thick and thin.

Tina and I were married in Burgaw, North Carolina, on March 13, 1982, in a formal Marine wedding ceremony, complete with dress blue uniforms and the traditional swords crossed overhead. Tina's family attended along with some of my Marine brothers. The Marines were now, Semper Fi, my extended family. They were my brothers who would always have my back and their attendance meant the world to me. It was unforgettable. It was perfect. More importantly, our ceremony was so incredibly blessed by the presence of God. I was so moved, I almost fell apart and wept. I had never dreamed of being so proud and happy in all my life! I had never dreamed of experiencing such feelings of being unconditionally loved and respected.

Oh, what a feeling!

As I am writing this book, I am happy and proud to say that, as of last March, Tina and I have been happily married for thirty-four years. We are also the devoted parents of four terrific adult children all of whom Tina home schooled. Every one of them is a fine upstanding citizen of this great country and a responsible, productive member of society. My children, in turn, have given us three incredible grandchildren, further proof of how the Lord continues to bless our union.

Tina, my children and grandchildren are my greatest joy and my most valuable assets. The comfort and love we give one another make our lives worth living. If it weren't for them, all my accomplishments, including my financial success, would be meaningless.

It's sad, but too many ambitious entrepreneurs and business people today mistake financial success with true success in life. Men, in particular, are often confused about this. Such individuals assume that if they acquire lots of money and amass the external trappings of great wealth, they will be able to attract beautiful, loving women, hundreds of loyal friends and social prestige. The popular press and media reinforce and promulgate this lie.

For it is a lie and if taken as the truth and pursued ruthlessly and relentlessly, people who fall for it will one day wake up with ashes in their mouths, surrounded by parasites, including members of their own families, that they can't trust.

No, as the saying goes: money cannot buy you love or happiness. Real gratification and contentment are to be found only in a rich and loving family life and within a loyal circle of true friends, people who will always stand by you, come what may, regardless of reversals of fortunes, debilitating illness and so on.

Such enduring relationships require abiding commitment and limitless forgiveness, in fact, the divinely inspired forgiveness Jesus demonstrated throughout His life on earth. There is no question but that people will disappoint you and let you down, and often when you need them the most. They are only human. But it is critical to forgive and forget their flaws and failings if you would lead a happy, satisfying life.

Tina and I faced this challenge directly and talked it through early in our marriage. Something happened right under our noses that forced the issue. After a long and happy marriage, to everyone's surprise and dismay, Tina's parents went through an ugly protracted divorce. It was an event so shocking, painful and disruptive to the entire family that it took years and a saintly depth of forgiveness for all of us to move on without anger and bitterness.

In the middle of this confusing, heartrending mess, Tina and I had a discussion and came to an agreement that further cemented and guaranteed our sacred wedding vows. We pledged to each other that the word divorce would not be in our vocabularies and would never be mentioned in our home. We resolved firmly that our union as man and wife would truly last until "death do us part." This lifetime promise, a private and personal reaffirmation of our matrimonial promises, admitted of no "if, ands or buts."

During the thirty-four years that we have lived together as man and wife, Tina and I have had many personal and financial disappointments and challenges, and we have suffered and survived serious illnesses and health scares when we thought one or the other of our lives was over. We have been through bankruptcies as a result of employee duplicity and betrayal, we have endured smear campaigns conducted by vindictive disgruntled employees that damaged our company's reputation, but never, not once, have we wavered or failed to support and encourage each other in dark times. In good times and bad, we have always shown loving respect and consideration for each other, whether in the privacy of our own home or in public.

I'm convinced this is the only way to go as a married couple, the only way to achieve happiness and contentment as man and wife, whatever you do, wherever you are. In fact, I highly recommend it!

Giving Up My Life's Career Ambition

"Change before you have to."

—Jack Welch

Chapter 26

Giving Up My Life's Career Ambition

After adjusting to my spiritual and matrimonial transformations, now with the new responsibility of providing for a wife and attending church on a regular basis, I soon realized that I had several serious conflicts and inconsistencies in my life. These needed to be addressed and resolved without delay.

I was trained by the Marines to be a killing machine, and so I had always aspired to eventually join the Federal Bureau of Investigation or the Central Intelligence Agency to work in counter-guerrilla operations or in a terrorist counter-tactics unit. I knew I had the necessary credentials for law enforcement because wholly unsolicited I was offered a position with the Pender County, North Carolina, Sheriff's Department as soon as I got out of the Marines. This once would have been flattering and the job offer appealing to me, but now I felt a hesitation, a check in my spirit. I did not know if it was the voice of God talking to me, but I felt an inner wrestling against following this path, a deep resistance to undertaking a violent line of work. I could not figure it out at the time, but my life was going in an entirely different direction.

It was a tough and confusing time. Martial arts and law enforcement had been career interests that I had wanted to pursue since I was just seven years old. It had become a major drive and obsession in my life. I had sold my soul for the purpose of killing and taking down the bad guys. Then, one day while I wrestled with the scripture that says, "Thou shall not kill," I fell on my face and wept before the Lord.

I sensed the leading of God in my life and felt Him calling me to give up the routine practice of carrying a gun and always working to improve my martial arts skills. Yet I just could not bring myself to make such a difficult sacrifice. A career in specialized law enforcement was my lifelong dream, and giving up fighting just did not feel right to me or seem like a reasonable option. It had taken me years to get where I was now and to attain my present high level of skill. I was proud of myself and the persistence and talent that the achievement required. I did not want to lose my edge or regress from my high skill ranking.

Yet I had come to a confusing, paralyzing crossroads. After lots of prayers and careful consideration, I reluctantly decided not to follow the guilt-inducing whispers of my conscience. It was clear to me that I quite selfishly did not want to change and give up my dreams. It was a self-centered, ego-driven choice. Strangely, just as I made that decision, I felt God quickly pulling away from me. I felt like someone just shut off a spiritual faucet in my life. The next day I tried to pray but felt as if I were coming up against a brick wall. I sensed God was no longer there for me, gently guiding, protecting, and listening to my prayers. I strongly sensed something was very wrong, but I did not fully understand what.

A week passed, and I still could not feel the presence of God in my life anymore. I was worried for my soul and desperate to feel His holy presence again. I kept struggling with my own runaway sinful ambitions versus God's will for my life. This all happened about two weeks before the end of my enlistment in the Marines —yet another reason I was having this struggle. I had a serious choice to make: stay in the Marines to fulfill my own ambitions and most likely take a life or lives, or leave the Corps and fulfill God's plan for my life.

Repeatedly in my life, the same scenario has played out, situations in which I struggled with making an important decision of some type, and somehow fate stepped in and showed me the right answer, often through some internal or external event, and often making it seem obvious the entire time. This time was no exception, but it was at the cost of a heartbreaking and tragic lesson.

On the morning of October 23, 1983, we all awoke to the news.

Overnight, the Marine Corps barracks in Beirut, Lebanon had been bombed. Two hundred and forty-one brave Marines had been brutally killed. A lone suicide bomber had driven a water truck through the very light security at the barracks at that time and blown it up. The blast was so powerful that, to this day, it is still believed to be the largest man-made, non-nuclear explosion ever detonated.

It was devastating for all of us, and the level of death and carnage was just incomprehensible to me.

I was put on hold status, and for the time being, I no longer had a choice in the matter. I was now a Marine for as long as they felt they needed me.

I waited.

In the end, I felt I just could not allow myself to be put in the middle of, or be a part of such evil, death, and destruction anymore. A few very tense weeks went by during which I was on full readiness, my gear always at my side, just waiting for the possibility that I would be shipped out to Lebanon. However, not surprisingly, there were plenty of Marine volunteers just chomping at the bit to go to Beirut and deal with the situation.

Eventually, I was put back on regular duty status, opted for my discharge, and was released from my second family that to this day, I still love with all my heart, the United States Marine Corps.

Being back in civilian life was a huge adjustment after four years of being a Marine. Tina and I lived with her parents while I made the transition from Marine to civilian, and my first order of business was to find a job. The first job I had out of the Marines was as a grocery clerk for Scotchman's Grocery Store. Shortly after I started my job, Tina and I found a lovely apartment in Burgaw, North Carolina. It was small, but it was ours. We were poor, but happy. We didn't have much, but we had the most important thing: we had each other.

However, I still struggled terribly with the separation and emptiness I felt when I tried to pray. I didn't know how to resolve the conflicts I had with what I wanted to do and what I felt God wanted me to do with my life. Eventually, my struggle and anguish brought me to the point of surrender, and I finally said "Yes" to Him.

"All right," I told God, "I surrender martial arts, my desire to work in law enforcement, and every other desire for my life."

I went home and removed of all my martial arts equipment and my weapons collections. After I cleaned house and made up my mind to do whatever He wanted me to do, I entered back into prayer, and an overwhelming presence of His glory and comfort greeted me. I wept like a baby, and my whole life seemed to take on a completely new meaning.

Some time later, God spoke to my heart more about being a witness to the power and glory by which He had saved me from myself, and released me from the hurt and pain that had been visited on me from my earliest memories.

I gladly accepted the challenge and told anyone who would listen, and some that evidently didn't want to, about my relationship with Jesus. However, to my shock and disappointment, I quickly found out that most other people were not as excited about Jesus as I was. With the dramatic change I had undergone in my own life, I just could not understand why no one would want to experience what I felt. I needed to share it with everyone. I wanted everyone to share in the peace, comfort, and joy of a close relationship with my Lord, Jesus Christ.

After about six weeks at Scotchman's, although they loved the job I did, my work ethic, and they liked me personally, they told me that unfortunately, they had to let me go for preaching too much on the job. In fact, all three of the jobs I got after my discharge resulted in termination for preaching too much Jesus.

It was very discouraging to keep being fired from my jobs for preaching Jesus, while still outworking everyone around me and trying to set a good example.

Yet, honestly, I should have known better, because sometime before my discharge from the Marines and my employment at Scotchman's, I'd had a rough introduction to the risks of preaching on the job. While I was deployed on an assignment in Japan, I was court-martialed and stripped of my rank for preaching on the job. I had been warned several times by the

Commanding Officer, but somehow, I could not restrain myself and stop talking about Jesus.

The court-martial judgment was eventually reversed in my favor, and my rank was restored. I should have learned my lesson from that difficult incident, but I didn't. It was too late for me. For by then I was a Christian through and through, inspired by my faith to spread the Good News everywhere I went to everybody I encountered.

I felt God wanted me to be the best example of a righteous Christian that I could be, which meant working hard and being diligent. I just had a really a hard time not sharing with people what I felt was the greatest experience of my life. I wanted everyone to have what I had, and I was not shy in the least bit in telling people about it.

Therefore, my next job was a major step up from a grocery clerk and actually wound up being my introduction to the construction business, a business I immediately fell in love with. It came to pass when, by a stroke of luck, I secured a job as an installer at Country Fair Mobile Homes. When someone bought a new mobile home or doublewide, we delivered it to the buyer, set it up, and checked it out entirely to ensure that everything worked properly. I just loved my new job, and the pay was a huge step up for me. However, I still could not stop myself from preaching about Jesus constantly to anyone and everyone I encountered. Once again, although my bosses at Country Fair Mobile Homes really liked me and I worked incredibly hard and did an excellent job for them, they still felt my incessant promotion of Jesus and the Christian faith was offensive to many customers and was costing them sales. Since I could not refrain from preaching because it was beyond my control, they soon became convinced that for the sake of their bottom line, they just had to let me go.

I ended up taking a significant pay cut when, after searching for several months for a new position, I took a job pushing grocery carts for Wilson's Grocery for only $420 a month. With dizzying speed, I had gone from being one of the most highly trained, highly skilled snipers in the Marine Corps, one of the most dangerous men in the world, to being a bag boy at a small grocery store in North Carolina and preaching Jesus to anyone who would listen. What a transformation. It was at times disorienting. Nevertheless, I was happier than I had ever been in my life. Everywhere I went, I told people about the power of the Holy Ghost.

Their individual reactions varied widely: responses ranged from annoyance, disgust, derisive contempt and laughter, ridicule, speechless awe, sneering disbelief, to total outright rejection. You name it. Yet I know I touched hearts. I know I brought many sensitive souls to the Lord.

Shortly after signing on with Wilson's Grocery, unaccountably, miracles suddenly seemed to start happening for me all the time, the biggest of which would come soon and it would turn out to be a major, life-saving event.

My sweet wife Tina had been gaining a belly for quite a while, and we were both ecstatic, assuming that she was pregnant with our first child. We were so thrilled, felt so blessed that we were going to have a baby. True, on $105 a week, we didn't have much money to spare, and my brother-in-law had recently wrecked my only car, so we had no money or transportation to go to a doctor for check-ups along the way.

But we both had what mattered most of all. For we both had a strong, rock-solid faith in God and so just had complete faith that the pregnancy would be okay. A little over eight months after we noticed the weight gain, we scraped together some money and decided we should, as responsible new parents, get to the hospital to make sure the baby was all right.

Once there, we were both shaken to the core when to our total shock, the doctor told us my wife wasn't pregnant at all. No, we listened in horror as he announced that instead, the abdominal swelling was a large mass cancerous tumor, and Tina had only three weeks to live.

This bad news came out of nowhere and was completely devastating to both of us. It hit us like a bomb. I can't begin to describe the sickening roller coaster of feelings we both went through after hearing the doctor hand us this "death sentence." It was not an easy thing for either of us to accept. The fear, anger, frustration, and sadness we cycled through were almost unbearable. We both felt betrayed.

We couldn't afford the hospital, and Tina wanted to be at home for her final days anyway, so we went back home and spent every possible minute together. I prayed a lot throughout those days. A few nights after we got home, Tina went into cardiac arrest, and as I picked up her little ninety-one-pound body and performed CPR, I prayed harder than I had ever prayed in my short Christian life. By the grace of God, I was able to bring her back with the CPR, and we got her to the hospital again, but it was evident that her time was drawing near.

After they got her stabilized at the hospital, I got her back home and did all I could do for her, which meant make her as comfortable as I could.

194

I watched her lie on her deathbed in that room for the next three days until, on the third day, something inexplicable happened.

I suddenly felt an overwhelming energy and power engulf the room. It wasn't something you could see; it was something you felt very intensely, and there was no mistaking it. An extremely powerful, pure, limitless energy force came flooding through the room, and then somehow, some way, a divine power instantly healed my wife right before our eyes. It was the most incredible manifestation of God's healing power anyone could imagine and impossible to describe.

Being a new Christian, I had no idea God could or would do such things. I was speechless, literally dumbstruck. I had thought those things only happened back in antiquity in Biblical times if they had happened at all. I realized that I had doubted Jesus' willingness to intervene in contemporary lives. I was wrong.

I quickly realized that I had tapped into a power, an eternal active, loving presence that could and would do anything for his devout followers. Yet this was only the beginning. The more I prayed, fasted, and sought Him, the more stupefying, supernatural things I saw happen. Although I had initially felt as though I had heroically sacrificed so much by giving up all my life's dearest ambitions, Jesus now gave me new inspiration and hope in this life. I no longer seemed to need those things that had once seemed so important to me. I was, true to say, no longer the major concern or center of my life. With this realization, a great burden was lifted from me, and scales were lifted from my eyes. Finally, I was free, yes, free from my selfish self.

My dear Lord also gave me back my beautiful wife, who is still healthy and cancer-free to this very day, and for that I will always be humbly and eternally grateful.

Becoming an Entrepreneur

"Success is going from failure to failure without loss of enthusiasm."

—Winston Churchill

Chapter 27
Becoming an Entrepreneur

After what I had witnessed with my wife Tina, I was totally enthralled by the seemingly limitless possibilities of my new life and engrossed with my dynamic spiritual relationship with God. I was filled with limitless zest and endless energy to discover God's will for me and wanted to follow his marching orders to the letter. My zeal for Jesus was all-consuming. I could hardly contain my excitement over what God had disclosed to me and what He had done for me, a sinner and so unworthy.

I went back to work, my faith and enthusiasm renewed by what had happened to my wife. Sure, the job provided pitiful earnings, but I was the happiest person in the world. Finding God's favor in my life was worth more than any amount of money or position. It put a bounce in my step and motivated me to become the best bag boy that grocery store ever had. Everywhere I went, I told people about the power of the Holy Ghost and what He did for my life. After Tina's amazing recovery, miracles seemed to happen all the time.

Once again, it was too much for some people, and I admit I probably overdid it, but after what I had seen and experienced with my darling wife, I didn't care what people thought. I simply had to tell everybody. I had to tell the world!

So, cut to the chase, after losing my third job for talking too much about Jesus, one of the elders in our church told me that God had dealt powerfully with her about having me start my own business. I was somewhat taken aback by this since I only had about fifteen dollars to my name, my car was wrecked, and I was on food stamps. What's more, I did not know anything about owning or running a business. This holy and kind woman earnestly pushed me, and she pushed really hard. She looked me in the eye, smiled faintly and plainly said, "The Lord has dealt with me about your future. Fast, watch and pray. Trust that He will answer you in His time."

Since I had no other job offers or opportunities, I thought about maybe cleaning windows for a living, as I had done as a kid in Seattle. So I took the fifteen dollars I had and bought several squeegees and a white bucket. I sawed off an old broomstick pole and turned it into a squeegee pole for reaching the higher windows. I made up some cards and set out on my adventure.

I walked house to house, being careful to only pick one-story homes because I didn't have a ladder. I walked for weeks without getting a single job. Then one day, I saw a modest and very nice looking, two-story home and decided to take a gamble.

I knocked on the door, made my little speech about my new services in town, and asked the lady for her business. She watched me patiently as I gave her my pitch and to my great relief, she smiled and then agreed to let me wash all her windows. I had finally landed my first job. My next question to her was if she had a ladder to get to the second floor of the house; when she said yes, I was in business.

I made $145 from that first job. With that money in hand, I immediately went to the hardware store and bought a six-foot wooden ladder. Now I really was in business. From that point on, I walked all over town cleaning windows with that six-foot wooden ladder on my shoulder, white bucket, and a sawed-off broomstick in my hand.

Soon afterward, I got my second job. I also put that money right back into my business by printing business cards and yellow flyers, and I bought more equipment.

I got up no later than 7 a.m. every morning and hit the ground running, whether I had a job or not. If I didn't have a job that day, I hit the street anyway in search of one, and I canvassed neighborhoods block by block, knocking on all doors until I had found one. As soon as I was done with the job, I knocked on more doors.

I kept getting more and more jobs. I refined my sales pitch and became more confident in my ability to get work and do excellent work. The excellent results of my strenuous efforts showed, and the jobs started coming in more regularly. Soon, what had started as a trickle of jobs, became a steady stream of jobs, and then a flood of work.

I worked harder than I ever had in my life just to keep up with it all. In fact, I never stopped working. I began to realize, however, that the growth of the business and the business itself was starting to suffer because dynamics were going on that I didn't fully understand. I knew I simply had to learn more about running and operating a business. When I wasn't actually cleaning windows, I read books on how to run a business. I also hired my brother-in-law to help me wash windows, and from that point on, things moved along very quickly.

I looked for ways to expand my business and quickly realized that car lots offered a unique opportunity for window washing work, as well as many other businesses, such as banks and any business with storefront windows. I also realized that repeat contracts were the way to go, jobs that would repeat on a frequent and regular basis. The more of those I could get, the bigger my bottom line, so I spent more and more time getting more and more jobs with local businesses, and grew my workforce to meet the increasing demand for my services.

The other thing I quickly realized was that to grow the business and make more money, I had to diversify and expand my services; offering janitorial services was a logical offshoot to what we were already doing. It was magic.

I started hiring more and more employees, buying more and more equipment, then more and more vehicles. Hiring more employees was the critical step in expanding and growing the business into a million-dollar company. I learned the more employees I had, the more money my company generated. This was true in any business.

"Spiderman" Gets His Name

"Whatever it takes to find the real you, don't be daunted if the rest of the world looks on in shock."

—Stephen Richards

Chapter 28
"Spiderman" Gets His Name

By this time, my company had come a long way from that humble, two-story home that had been my very first job and had expanded into some exciting new services. I was now doing commercial window cleaning on high-rise, "suicidal" buildings throughout all the major cities in North Carolina.

Doing "suicidal" buildings may seem crazy, but when I was making thirty to fifty thousand dollars a year per building, just for the cleaning, and each one took only about a week to do, you can see the method to my madness.

Using my Marine Corps rappelling training and experience, I had designed my own rigging systems for scaling up and down the sides of these massive buildings. At the same time, I branched out even further and expanded into other essential services that I could perform while I was on the side of the building, such as caulking and sealing windows, construction repairs, and other routine maintenance.

Shortly after I started doing the "suicidal" buildings, the news media noticed what had become somewhat of an overnight local sensation and nicknamed me "Spiderman."

My unique and versatile means of scaling virtually impossible structures with ropes, suction cups, PR-3 pulley rappel systems, specialized wall braces, and several of my own custom-designed wall walking systems had gotten everybody's attention.

My customers and the news media seldom referred to me by my real name and numerous newspaper articles and TV news reports referred to me as "Spiderman." Articles such as "Spiderman Shows Deputies the Ropes," when I trained the SWAT team in Pensacola, or "At Work, 'Spiderman' Relies on Ropes, Jesus" were common.

That unique nickname would end up staying with me forever and even become part of both my business and my real name. I actually changed my legal name to add "Spiderman" to it. Today, my real name on my driver's license reads "Spiderman Scott Mulholland."

Learning About Business

the Hard Way

"Challenges are what make life interesting and overcoming them is what makes life meaningful."

—Joshua J. Marine

Chapter 29

Learning About Business the Hard Way

During this time, my father-in-law had moved and had been living in Florida for a while, creating a strong temptation for us to move down there too. After making several casual visits, we had pretty much convinced ourselves that we wanted to live in the Sunshine State permanently, and so we decided to make the move.

It didn't take long for me to sell my company in North Carolina to a nice enough man, and we packed up the house and rented a place in Pensacola, Florida, near my father-in-law. We enjoyed our new life in Florida as I quickly built a new type of company — Spiderman's Professional Services.

As the name implied, Spiderman's Professional Services was a somewhat new concept of the old business, in which I expanded my services and offerings to include professional construction, maintenance, and janitorial services, as well as the traditional window cleaning duties.

Things started out slowly at first, which I fully expected, but at least, this time I had the money to buy starter equipment. I knew what I was doing now. I knew my target clients and how to get them.

Car lots, banks, any and every high-rise building I could find, literally any business that had windows, I hit them all. Soon, I was on my way, and it was a very exciting time.

That was until the nice enough man who had bought my business in North Carolina, turned out to be a crook. I had sat across a table from this man and his attorney, looked over a 25-page stack of papers and contracts, signed where they told me to and then took a large sum of money they had just given me for my business. I smiled and figured that was how it was done and that I had just made a good business deal.

I was very proud of myself, and we were quickly off to Florida, never giving the sale of the business a second thought. I was young, inexperienced and naïve.

About eight months after we moved to Pensacola, I started getting past due and collection notices from suppliers and other businesses in North Carolina. It turned out that, when this nice enough man took over the business, he didn't file the transfer of ownership paperwork with the state. Then he looted the company of all its cash, stole and liquidated all the assets, stopped paying the bills, the employees, and taxes. Almost a year after I had sold the company, everything legally defaulted back into my name.

The contracts I had signed with him were all meaningless; he had stripped everything out of the company, including the clients, and that's when all the bills on the trucks, equipment, and taxes found me in Florida. It was devastating to realize that I had been ripped off so badly and could not do anything about it.

I spent two years trying to grow the new business, while at the same time trying to pay back the IRS and bill collectors until we were finally forced into bankruptcy on the North Carolina business. I felt like such a failure, and my whole life turned upside down.

What do you do when something like that happens?

You surely don't waste time feeling sorry for yourself and let it slow you down or stop you. You do not use it as an excuse for not getting back up to pursue your passion and your dream. Yes, it is devastating when things like this happen, but you have to accept that it happened and immediately start moving forward again. Business is all about managing and handling risk and dealing with adversity. You cannot dwell on any type of major setback, or it will suck away all your passion and energy, and destroy any chance you have of being successful.

You have to take care of your health and live to fight another day. Then, go fight.

Therefore, what you do in a case like this is pick up the pieces again and start knocking on even more doors and working even harder.

That's exactly what I did, and once again, my new business in Florida took off and thrived. Trying to grow and expand the new business, while trying to pay off the debt from the bankruptcy at the same time, was very slow and tough, but I finally did it. In just four years of very hard work and never, ever giving up, Spiderman's Professional Services became a multi-million-dollar company, and I had paid back everyone I owed money, despite the bankruptcy, and plotted another course for my company.

I also hired an excellent corporate attorney and a business administrator.

The whole experience had really devastated me, but it had also been an incredible business learning experience, and this led me on another course. I began a journey as not only an entrepreneur and multi-million-dollar business owner, but I also became a true autodidact. Previously, I had self-taught myself everything I needed to know to run my business, but now my quest for knowledge became almost insatiable.

I spent day and night in the business section in bookstores and studied business until the late-night hours. I spent hours in prayer asking God to illuminate my mind and to not let me ever be so stupid as to let someone rip me off again. I had realized that I was street smart, but not business smart... not yet.

I also realized I was the only person that could change that. I was the only person who could help myself. I realized that the more skills I had and the more I knew, the more money I could make and the less chance someone would ever have of getting one over on me again.

Over the past thirty years, I invested over three-hundred-thousand dollars in my personal education and have flown all over America attending schools, trade shows, and certification courses, learning both business skills and the industry of construction. I went on to further diversify my education, experience, and skill sets by becoming certified in construction forensic investigations, building science, and many other specialties. As I did in the Marines, I became a master at everything that I could find and bring to the table that could possibly help me accomplish my mission.

Losing It All Should Not Stop You

"Never, never, never give up."

—Winston Churchill

Chapter 30

Losing It All Should Not Stop You

For the next seventeen years, my multi-million-dollar company grew and thrived, and I kept learning more and more skills to grow as a person and business. For seventeen years, life was good, and my family and I were able to enjoy the fruits of my labors as I built an exciting, successful business. Yet once again, I faced losing everything at the hands of another.

In this case, it all began when I fired the general contractor over my construction division for unethical behavior. This really devastated me personally, especially taking into consideration how well we had taken care of him. He had a six-figure income, a truck, health and life insurance with the liberty to grow and push the construction side of our business the way he saw fit.

The decision to fire him was crushing to me personally, but nowhere near as difficult as the events that followed.

We sought out another qualifier on a job we were doing and, in the process, the deceitful former employee was turned in for contracting without a license and failure to pull a permit on a project he'd previously overseen for my company. Because I was the owner of the business, the District Attorney actually issued arrest warrants for me personally, and for the first time in my life, I was arrested for a crime. Humiliated and shocked, I sought out the people involved and the charges that were levied against us. It seemed the DA had received anonymous complaints from several people about our company. This was shocking to me because, in seventeen years, we had never received so much as a single Better

Business Bureau complaint, and we have serviced several hundred clients each year. We had twenty-seven billboards, a radio show called "Ask the Expert" and a TV show on construction technology. How could we go from being one of the premier specialty contractors in the state of Florida to being a lowlife arrested as a criminal?

The plot thickened as my clients called me to report that a DA was soliciting them to testify against me. They said the DA offered them money for their testimony and would refund any amount of money they had paid me for work. This time, I had lawyers, but when challenged, the DA simply said it was compensation. We called it extortion.

Eventually, only one person over the next six months came forward to testify. Ultimately, I ended up paying restitution and pleaded no contest to the misdemeanor charge of operating without a license and failure to pull a permit. I took responsibility for the misdeeds of my former employee, and this time I suffered through a terrible personal bankruptcy stemming from the state attorney's unwillingness to let me continue operating my business.

We fought and eventually found out that his star witness had been none other than my former general contractor whom I had fired. When the DA's office figured out the connection, all charges were conveniently and quietly dropped with no official explanation. All the spurious charges and allegations just disappeared, abruptly swept under the carpet as if the whole thing had never happened.

However, as far as my reputation and that of my business were concerned, the damage had been done, and it was irrevocable. Once again, I had been totally wiped out financially, and my company's once good name was now associated with the whole mess and badly tarnished. In every facet of my financial and business life, I felt damaged beyond repair.

Everything I had spent seventeen years strenuously building had been shattered right before my eyes by irresponsible legal actions of the authorities and maliciously engineered events by unethical former employees. The sequence of events that had caused this catastrophe was completely beyond my control.

This time, I really felt violated and mistreated. How can such a bad thing happen to someone who had done everything in his power to be honest and ethical for so many years?

I had a wife and kids who depended on me, so I had no time to mourn my losses or to dwell on the fairness of this situation. It was what it was, and I would just have to suck it up, shake it off, and deal with it. So, down at the mouth, but still resolute, I picked up what I had left after this disaster, which was about five-hundred dollars, and launched out once again to rebuild my business and regain our family income.

Starting over was incredibly difficult this time, especially after seeing almost all my belongings taken away in the personal bankruptcy. I watched my family suffer humiliation and troubling insecurity as a result, and it nearly killed me. My poor children lost so much during this period, security, confidence, and their natural optimism. Such events cause the worst kind of heartache and remorse in any parent.

Nevertheless, this time, by fully understanding the basic principles of business and by protecting my health through the nightmare, I launched US Building Consultants and grew it to over a million dollars in revenue in its first two years.

Coming out of personal bankruptcy and becoming a millionaire again in less than two years was not an easy task, let me tell you. Furthermore, it took everything in my being to forgive the callous, indifferent people involved and not file civil lawsuits against everyone who had been involved in destroying my life's work.

I Could Have Made Excuses, but I Became Successful Instead

"If you don't have confidence, you'll always find a way not to win."

—Carl Lewis

Chapter 31

I Could Have Made Excuses, but I Became Successful Instead

There is an old saying that goes, "Success is the sweetest form of revenge," or something to that effect. I honestly don't know if this was a factor in motivating me so intensely in my drive to rise out of the ashes of my former hard-won prosperous life and become successful once more. On a subconscious level, it may very well have been a factor, but if it wasn't, given my childhood, it surely should have been.

I could have let my nightmare of a childhood leave me bitter and beaten after this crushing business defeat. Actually, I could have let these disastrous reversals ruin my entire life, and become completely consumed with anger and obsessed with obtaining revenge of some kind. It would have been a great and justifiable excuse to give in to those toxic feelings and to never try again at life; it would have been all too easy to cave into bitterness, depression and despair.

But I couldn't allow myself to give into those negative, self-destructive urges. For me, it would have been a total cop-out, and, after all I'd been through, after all I'd survived and all I'd overcome, it was never an option.

Once I got a chance to get on my feet by joining the Marines, I had found my inner strength and my true self. The experiences I went through growing up, each one of them, only served to make me a stronger person, a better Marine, and in the end a better man and businessman.

After the physical and mental abuse I received during my childhood and growing up, Marine Corps boot camp was tough but much easier for me than for just about anyone else I knew there. I could take what they dished out and perform my job well without fearing them. On top of it, even though I had many moments when I felt like that twelve-year-old in a nineteen-year old's body, I can look you straight in the eye and tell you I was an outstanding Marine, and today, I am afraid of no man, and never will be.

Compared to hiding from kidnappers inside a dumpster all night on Seattle's skid row and covering up in boxes inside dumpsters through freezing Seattle winters, taking six hours to slowly crawl on my belly in a ghillie suit, through hundreds of enemy soldiers, to stalk and kill an "enemy" captain, was a picnic.

I could have let getting ripped-off on the sale of my first business be an excuse for me to give up on owning a business; I could have not paid off the debts. It would have been a very understandable excuse; it would have been easy. But that would have been an even bigger cop-out.

Why? Because, by this time, I knew exactly what I was capable of, and what it took to start and run a million-dollar business. I knew that the people to whom my company owed money also had businesses to run, with hard-working employees to pay, and as a man, I was now responsible for those debts.

I could have given up when a man whom I considered a friend and to whom I had been very generous betrayed me and tried to destroy my business after I fired him. Nevertheless, after building two million-dollar companies from the ground up by myself, the third time I was in familiar

217

territory. I could have used it as an excuse to just take a day job somewhere and given up altogether on owning a business. I could have taken all the skills I had learned running my first company and gone to work for a company with benefits and a retirement plan. I could have turned my back on God and gone into law-enforcement. I had been offered a job with the Pender County Sheriff's Dept., and Ex-Marines with a rank of E-5 or above, which I was, were an automatic hire with the Florida Highway Patrol.

I became successful because I didn't take any of those "easy-out" routes. I would not let what happened to me become a lame excuse for not going after what I honestly wanted to do. More importantly, I became successful by staying true to my most deeply held beliefs, by never turning my back on the Lord and my Christian values and faith. I never let anything kill my passions in life and my drive for becoming who I want to be.

Find your own passion in life and in business, and once you do, don't ever give it up.

Get a good education, read, study more, then read and study some more. Become an autodidact and plunge into the depth of what possesses you on the inside. Tap into that God-given drive and gift you have, that vision and dream that sits in silent obscurity. Go find it and possess it no matter what happens, no matter the cost, no matter who strikes out at you, no matter who or what you lose in the course of your life. Whatever happens to you in life, no matter the adversity, the financial or emotional challenge, don't ever stop going after what you have been destined to accomplish.

You cannot kill something that will not die. Bottom line: Success is simply a matter of refusing to give up when others have.

Unfortunately, bad things do happen to good people, but when bad things happen in your life or your business, you must get over them and move on.

Stay away from idiots and negative people.

Stay away from people who constantly seek out some kind of drama in their lives. They will only suck you in and make you play a part in their drama. Don't be fooled into thinking you are helping someone by playing in his or her drama. They live for the drama and they can't function in our society without constant drama. If you want people to be more successful than they want to be, you are wasting your time.

Always get yourself strong and financially sound first, then you will have the time and resources to help those around you.

Don't let people bleed your resources; you will be left with nothing and you really cannot help anyone else if you can't help yourself.

Be smart — pay yourself first.

Always go the extra mile and when in doubt, always err on the side of your heart, not your brain. That way, even if you are proven wrong, you will know that you did what you felt was right.

No, I am not sure if the desire to exact revenge for my miserable childhood was a motivating factor in my insatiable drive for success. Yes, it could have been and probably should have been. However, I can tell you this for sure: the taste of revenge may be sweet, but the smell and taste of success are much sweeter, and once you've tasted success in your life, you'll never stop wanting more.

The Best Part of My Story

"They talked in the shorthand of old friends and shared memories."

—Dee Henderson, Before I Wake

Chapter 32
The Best Part of My Story

There is much more to my story that I've held off relating to you until now. All of it is equally important to what I've covered so far, but it deserves separate treatment because it is of a more personal and inter-personal nature. In fact, as it all transpired over many years, it seemed that it paralleled my public life for a long time without intersecting or merging with the main goals and events of my life.

The fact is, however, that in telling my rough and tumble life story here, I have saved the sweetest and best for last. The main themes of this part of my story are the human capacity for compassion and forgiveness. Without receiving the kind and very concerned intervention, consideration, and charity of remarkable adults outside of my family all along the way, I have to candidly confess that I would not have survived and lived to overcome my horrible childhood circumstances, let alone achieved the degree of success that I have today.

I will begin with my earliest memory of this. When I was two-years-old and still in the custody of my parents in Seattle, a kind, caring neighborhood woman, a good mother and foster mother herself, took me in when my mother kicked me out, or I ran away. I've mentioned her earlier in this book, but I feel I have not done justice to all that she did for me or adequately expressed my deep gratitude for her help after losing my Mom at four years-old. This neighborhood woman would many times feed me, clothe me, and care for me as if I were her own child. I played with her children, her daughter Debbie especially, who was my age.

Emotionally starved and craving safety, security and a mother's love, I quickly settled into the new domestic arrangements at this dear woman's house and merged with her family in her warm and always welcoming home. My Dad seemed to tacitly approve of this arrangement and looked the other way because he worked twelve hour days delivering milk for a dairy at the time, and he found it nearly impossible to adequately provide for me and all my brothers.

Almost every afternoon this kind generous woman, my new Mom, would call me in from playing outside and serve me fresh baked homemade chocolate chip cookies. The practice became a sweet daily ritual for the two of us. As I enjoyed her delicious cookies, she and I would chat about things and exchange jokes and stories. Those are still such wonderfully happy memories. I treasure them beyond words. In no time at all, I was calling this sweet woman "Mom." As you will perhaps recall, her real name is Kathy Hoppenrath. I am so deeply and profoundly grateful for everything she did for me. She went above and beyond normal human compassion and decency.

This comforting arrangement continued on and off until, first, my real Mom, then my Dad, lost legal custody of my four brothers and me, and we were put into the foster system by the courts.

In recent years, I have made a conscious effort to reconnect with the extraordinary people like Kathy who helped me as a child. Over time, Kathy and Joe Schemnitzer both reached out to me via social media. Reconnecting with them gave me a longed-for opportunity to thank and honor those who had, in effect, saved my life. I was consumed with gratitude and desire to show them that I hadn't let them down. Because of their priceless help, I had indeed made something of myself. Against all odds, but only because of their remarkable charity and generosity in reaching out to me, I had, at last, amounted to something. I had succeeded beyond my wildest dreams, and their efforts had not been in vain.

I found that Kathy Hoppenrath was still living in Seattle and made a trip out there to visit her. My reunion with her was joyful and loud! Kathy's daughter, Debbie, surprised me and joined her mom for our reunion. We had a lot of catching up to do, a lifetime's worth! It was absolutely unbelievable! Kathy showed me touching photographs of the years I spent in her motherly care. When I later showed them to Tina, it was an eye-opener. Until she saw those photos, most of what Tina used to visualize my early years was based on oral recollections. Kathy, Debbie and I talked non-stop for hours, eager to get up to date as quickly as we could. What a tender, heartrending reunion we had. As we chatted away about everything under the sun in no particular order, it became crystal clear to me that the bond between us was still strong, intimate and very much alive. The visit left us energized and exhilarated. Today, Tina and I still stay in touch with Kathy by phone and email, and I look forward to the opportunity to visit her when I find myself in Seattle again.

More happy, energizing reconnections swiftly followed. The good man "Joe" who finally got me out of the dumpster on Seattle's skid row beat me to the punch in reestablishing our communication. This is the fine man who coached me out of the dumpster, ignored my insulting suspicions about his kind behavior, and without any encouragement from me, insisted on helping me improve my life, no matter what I said or did. You will recall that he took me to his home, introduced me to his terrific non-

223

judgmental parents, gave me a clean place to sleep, fed me—and got me into the Marines! This great guy even paid my bus fare back to Seattle when I got in trouble with the Las Vegas police on something minor. They called him from Las Vegas and said I had claimed Joe was my big brother. The police said they'd let me go if Joe sent them bus fare to ship me home! He did so pronto, and I was off the hook.

Joe also, God bless his great big heart, paid off all my outstanding traffic tickets, parking fines and fines for other infractions so that my record was clean and I could legally join the military.

Joe Schemnitzer had been so patient with my seventeen-year-old limitations, neuroses, and ignorance when he reached out to me that, looking back on it today, I'm amazed and more than a little embarrassed at my crazy doubts, suspicions and rude behavior at that time. It is just staggering what he did for me despite my initial rejections of his attempts to help me. I would never be where I am today if it were not for Joe. It's impossible to show enough gratitude for all he did for me, impossible for me to ever repay him. All I can do is love him without question, thank him constantly and continue to strive to be the good person he hoped I would be.

But this is nothing new, really. Even back when I joined the Marines, many years ago, one of my chief ambitions, something that really motivated me, was already my strong desire to make Joe and his parents proud of me. I hope I succeeded.

At any rate, while I was casting about for a way to contact Joe, he found me. Joe had run across a magazine article mentioning me which included a photograph of me receiving an award. We had not communicated in many, many years, and had lost track of each other. When I enlisted in the Marines, Joe and his dear mother regularly wrote me encouraging newsy letters. But when I was discharged and married Tina, our correspondence gradually tapered off.

Nevertheless, after seeing the article about me in the magazine, Joe got in touch with us. Man, it was "old home week!" We talked our heads off trying to catch up as fast as we could. Both of our lives had changed so much that we had a lot of ground to cover. I was now the father of four adult children, the grandfather of three beautiful grandchildren, and a successful entrepreneur business owner. I had also received many professional accolades and had earned several professional degrees and certifications.

Joe, on the other hand, had suffered through a serious bout of cancer some years before and had nearly succumbed to it, as a matter of fact. It was so debilitating, and it made him so weak that he was sure that he was dying. In spite of his bleak assumptions and the dire medical prognosis the doctors gave him, Joe had somehow surprisingly recovered. After that bad health scare, he retired from his long-term career with Transamerica. As for his gig as a bar bouncer was concerned, I finally discovered that job had been only a temporary weekend gig which he had voluntarily given up when I was still living with him so that he could spend more time with me on weekends. He was worried that the bouncer job that he had was robbing me of the care and attention that I needed. He didn't think I was receiving the necessary adult supervision and encouragement that a kid with my warped background and deep emotional issues required to stay out of trouble.

225

Imagine that; such was the depth of his giving, his sincere concern for the welfare of an obnoxious street urchin previously unknown to him. Well, it was almost a spiritual solicitation for my well-being. In retrospect, I'm sure his actions were divinely inspired. There was just no end to what that man would do for me, no sacrifice he wouldn't make to help me.

Once we located Joe, without a thought about the expense and time involved, Tina and I traveled cross country to Seattle, just a few months before this writing, and had a long newsy visit with him. I simply cannot speak highly enough of my "big brother" Joe Schemnitzer. In so many ways, I owe him my life.

During our emotional and sometimes tearful reunion, Joe and I shared countless memories in rapid succession, both happy and sad, and he gave me a big collection of old photographs, some of which made me bawl like a baby, that he had saved of our times together. My mere eight months in his company so long ago had changed the course of my life, though as an adolescent at the time with only an immature grasp of the way the world works, it would take me years to wake up to what he had done for me and to fully appreciate its significance.

I can hardly express, even today, my overwhelming love and appreciation for Joe and all he did for me, now that I am finally at a stage of maturity at which I can grasp the immensity of his selfless actions on behalf of the poor dumb homeless street kid that I was at the time.

Finding and Forgiving My Mother

"Forgiveness is unlocking the door to set someone free and realizing you were the prisoner."

—Max Lucado

Chapter 33

Finding and Forgiving My Mother

Early in my life my mother had been ruled unfit to care for her children. She was, in fact, declared a danger to her children, and by a court-issued restraining order was forbidden to see us. Yet she repeatedly ignored the wishes of the court and would check in on us and contact us from time to time.

I both loved and feared my mother, particularly when she was drinking. Alcohol really changed her and turned her into a different person. While kind and responsible when she was sober, she was wildly unpredictable and prone to violent rages when inebriated. This behavior had gone on for years, and the police were always at our home responding to Dad's domestic violence calls, and eventually bringing with them grim-faced social workers and child advocates to investigate our living situation. Regardless of everything she had done, however, I refused to blame her and insisted on blaming the alcohol instead.

Despite all the terrible trouble alcohol caused in her life, for eventually she just lost everything because of her drinking, Mom would not and perhaps could not stop. But my needy love for her never lessened, and I clung to her with all my might, no matter how badly she hurt me emotionally and physically. When we were removed from her custody by the courts, and she lost all visitation rights to us, I was completely shattered and had what amounted to a nervous breakdown. The state agencies gave me a lot of psychiatric care and supervision over several years for my resulting emotional problems, but as I said earlier in this book, it was worthless and helped not at all.

No, even though we were, by law, forbidden to see each other, she remained a heartbreaking presence on the fringe of my life. She was still alluring to me because she symbolized love and gave me a source of protection and security. Always at a distance and never fully there for me, she watched silently from afar for the most part as I grew up. When I boarded the plane for San Diego to join the Marines, Mom was at the airport, kissed me good-bye and wished me good luck. By that time, I was nearly eighteen-years-old and had a little perspective on her behavior and the role her alcoholism played in determining how she would treat me, my brothers, sister, and my Dad.

Mom and I sporadically exchanged letters while I was in the Marine Corp. Yet our communication was inconsistent and eventually fell off. When at last I returned to the States and was stationed in North Carolina, I let her know where I was and, surprisingly, she visited me there a couple of times, beginning in 1986, after Tina and I were married.

During these years, I was noticing a new calm and stability in her deportment, a new serenity which puzzled me at first. It turned out that certain key developments had taken place in Mom's world that were perhaps the best things that could have happened to her and which maybe even saved her life. I know they saved our relationship as mother and son. First, Mom quit drinking and joined AA. The crushing burden of alcohol addiction, which has ruined so many lives, was finally lifted from her. In AA Mom found the information she needed to fight her slavery to alcohol, the unwavering support of other recovering alcoholics just like herself, and a proven rigorous recovery program that worked if you "worked" it.

Then, in God's own timing and by His good grace, Mom also found a suitable, sound and sober life partner, himself also a recovering alcoholic and in AA for years. Not only were they attracted to each other, but they deeply understood each other's struggles with the bottle and had experienced the destruction and ruin of their lives that long-term alcoholism inevitably brings. There was an instant attraction between the two of them that soon deepened into a profoundly important mutual understanding of each other's plight and hardships. Today they together keep each other on the straight and narrow while enjoying each other's loving company, mutual respect, and emotional support. They have now been married for over thirty years, and their union grows stronger with each passing day.

No coincidence, I suppose, that they have been faithful members of AA for about the same number of years.

In my view, this change in my mother is miraculous. You can't take back the damage that was done or erase the terrifying memories, for, unfortunately, they are permanent. But the healing and forgiveness that Mom's lifestyle changes have made possible have given our families a previously unimagined sense of peace and longed-for reconciliation.

George means the world to my Mom and they get along famously. She has finally found happiness in a marriage that was clearly blessed and meant to be. As I write this, I'm pleased to know that Mom is now a successful businesswoman, a talented artisan, who creates and markets her own handcrafted original work. She promotes her unique line of items at tradeshows and thanks God for this blessing every day.

I have visited and talked to my Mom more in the last few years than I believe I ever did previously in my whole life. We are closer than we have ever been and nearly all our recent memories are happy and joyful. We engage in no fault finding or recrimination over previous mistakes or hurts we have caused each other. AA has helped make it possible for Mom to be a new woman, a woman full of life, love, and laughter at the tender vital age of seventy-nine years young.

A really dramatic incident that pointedly demonstrated how far Mom and I had evolved in our mother-son relationship occurred on my 50th birthday, October 25, 2012. Unbeknownst to me, Tina made elaborate secret plans for a surprise birthday party for me to celebrate the occasion. She invited lots of our close friends, extended family members who lived out of state, key employees who were near and dear to me, and neighbors whom we were fond of. It was quite a large and boisterous crowd.

Of course, I was none the wiser and completely ignorant of what was going on behind the scenes. Always obsessed with the details of my work, business, and my faith activities as a devout Christian, I was probably the most easily distractible person on the planet earth. To say that I was focused like a laser on what I had to do to keep these three most important things in my life afloat is a gigantic understatement. With your nose always to the grindstone, you rarely look up, or from side to side, to check what else is going on in the world.

So it followed that Tina easily got me off the premises by persuading me to run some errands for her. She had planned everything carefully and

well, for there was ample time after the sun went down for the invitees to arrive, park and enter our home under cover of darkness. After the fact, as I reviewed the brilliantly devised fun we had at the "Surprise" Party, I remarked on Tina's cunning planning and precise calculations, and I concluded that no question and without a doubt, my wife herself would have made a great Marine. She had all the right stuff.

At last, when exactly according to plan, all the guests had arrived while I was away, Tina sent our daughter out to find me and bring me home for my big surprise.

When my daughter and I came back home, a riotous mob of smiling, high-fiving friends and relations greeted me in the great room, hollering, "Surprise! Surprise!" And believe me, it was a total surprise to me! It really knocked me back. I hadn't a clue that this was in the works. I had only expected and looked forward to a fun family birthday party at the kitchen table in the evening after everybody's workday was over.

Almost immediately after I got back home, I was hit by an even greater surprise. Unannounced and without a hint of possibility of such a thing, an unknown "someone" urgently rang the doorbell, almost as if this person was in trouble or had important news to convey to the residents of our home. At this disturbing sound, Tina, ever the perfect and attentive hostess, flew across the room to answer it and see what was what. When she did, she was so flabbergasted by what she saw outside on our front doorstep that she instantly slammed the door in the visitor's face and wide-eyed called for me in a shrill voice. "Come quick!" she said, pointing at the closed door.

Not knowing if she was responding to the sudden appearance of a friend or foe, I rushed through the puzzled, now quiet crowd to the front door. Then I gathered myself up, put on my tough guy face, and braced myself for whatever came next. With wide, uncomprehending eyes, Tina glanced up at me, smiled, and pointed to the door.

I slowly turned the doorknob and opened the door a crack. I couldn't believe what I saw. Standing on the front step in a pool of light was none other than my Mother!

She was smiling sweetly and had tears in her eyes. Her arms were sagging from the weight of many gift-wrapped boxes with photo albums stacked on top. She looked just great.

"Scottie," she said, grinning and calling me by my childhood name, "May I come in?"

True to say, this was the best birthday present I had ever received in my life, the surprise appearance of my beloved mother, who had flown all the way from Seattle, Washington, to Gainesville, Florida, to be with me on my Fiftieth Birthday! I was so overwhelmed by her unexpected appearance that I totally lost it and burst into tears.

Her happy presence and maternal charisma drew me to her like a magnet. I reached out, embraced her in a big bear hug, and helped her inside. In the bright foyer, I could see the crowd of well-wishers staring at us with silent questioning faces. I smiled broadly and announced proudly in a loud voice, "Hey, guys, this is my Mom! She flew in all the way from Seattle to be with us tonight to celebrate my birthday!" This news was followed by a long, deafening roar of applause that shook the house to its foundations.

What Excuses Are Holding You Back?

"He that is good for making excuses is seldom good for anything else."

—Benjamin Franklin

Chapter 34

What Excuses Are Holding You Back?

I'm sure my story has not always been the easiest thing for some folks to read; all the cruelty, bad behavior, and disappointment that it chronicles could easily have become too much for some sensitive personalities. Nevertheless, a true and accurate account of what I endured to get to where I am today is what I was aiming for, however disturbing and distasteful it happened to be. To tell the truth and enable others to overcome their disadvantages, it was essential to turn some stomachs and break some hearts with what have been the savage realities of my early life. If you would find satisfaction, joy, and beauty, if you would find enduring love and lifelong friends, if you would achieve financial success, you must accept the hard truth that life is tough, very often cruel and seemingly hopeless. You will never make it if you don't face it and embrace it for what it is and in spite of the overwhelming odds against you. Only then can you gather up your guts, believe in yourself, forge ahead, and so overcome whatever challenges and obstacles that stand in your way.

That means every day. All the time. Whatever happens. Remember: It's all up to you, and if I did it, you can too! Anyone equipped with these simple facts of life can be a success.

So, what's stopping you? Fear? Denial? Procrastination? Self-pity? Baloney! That dog won't hunt. If you cave into those ordinary everyday distractions, you're doomed. What do you have to lose by going for the gold instead? Loneliness? Poverty? Lack of self-esteem? Kick them to the curb and go for it!

Take the leap of faith! Jump! Trust me, you now have no legitimate excuse, and it's the only way to get ahead.

Let me repeat, you have no excuse. It's entirely up to you. Your future is not preordained by "fate," "the government," "your family" or anything else outside of your power. Believe in who you are and who and what you want to become and it will happen. The fact is, when properly viewed, you will discover that all of us harbor within ourselves a sleeping Superman or Spiderman waiting to be awakened and called into service to help us succeed and realize our goals.

As abrasive and distasteful as some parts of my story are, I hope I have made perfectly clear the grim reality of what happened to me as well as the unexpected, miraculous intervention of good people on my behalf that turned my life around. I admit, living through it wasn't easy and lots of what happened permanently damaged me in important ways. But my point here has been to show conclusively that if you keep the faith and persist in the face of whatever the odds you face, you can and you will make it. Keeping your eye on the goal, letting nothing deter you—those are within the power of every ordinary human being if only he or she receives an inkling of inspiration and support.

I am today myself living proof that you can overcome any disadvantage, injustice or economic hardship if you keep on keeping on. The world is full of good people who will reach out and help you in your distress, people like Kathy Hoppenrath and Joe Schemnitzer in my own life. Yet I believe it has been critical for me to not mince words and to tell

236

the raw truth about my life to show you what I have overcome to get where I am today.

Horrible, wasn't it? Sometimes disgusting, wasn't it? Heartbreaking too, wasn't it? Wake up and grow up. If I can do it, you can do too. Anyone can. My purpose in writing this book, as difficult, revealing and painful as it was in re-hashing my early life, was to demonstrate conclusively to others out there who are hurting and struggling as I did, that there is a way out of their troubles and seemingly hopeless situations. They too can survive, succeed and thrive.

There are probably millions of kids out on the streets right now with the same crippling, deforming disadvantages that I had as a kid. I want them to know they can succeed, they can overcome the odds, if they only believe in themselves, work hard and persist. Is there maybe something specific in your past that you feel is holding you back? Trust me, it's not real, it's a figment of your imagination, and it's not to be trusted. You can live in a graveyard of failure and excuses, or you can walk out, close the gate on all your failures and hardships behind you and start a new and exciting adventure of hopes and dreams.

The truth is that all our battles in life are fought and won or lost between our ears. If you are using an excuse of a past failure or event in your life as the cause of a current lack of success, I strongly advise you to find a dark room and lock yourself in it. Don't come out until you have carefully examined the very inside of your being, to the depths of your soul if need be.

You need to fully understand that you cannot be held hostage by your past, unless you, yourself, allow that to happen. By allowing the events of

237

the past to keep affecting you, you are thereby enabling them to hold you hostage. Wallowing in self-pity and feeling sorry for yourself are the most destructive and counter-productive time-wasters standing in the way of your future success.

All men and women fail. The great ones get back up.

No matter what failure, excuse or past event you have experienced that is hindering your future success or is holding you back, in reality, it has no real hold or bearing on your life, except for whatever power you are giving it between your ears.

Let go of the past, especially the people who have hurt you or tried in any way to destroy you.

Today, you can decide to make a change, but it all starts in your mind. You can decide in one moment to change your mind-set by letting go of your past and formulating a new one. You will be amazed how your body, mind, and spirit will change direction, just by changing your outlook on life.

Tony Robbins is probably one of the greatest personal development coaches of our time, and it is well worth the cost to attend one of his seminars if you can; it's a life-changing experience. He has impacted my life by many of his teaching and training courses over twenty-five years. Although Tony Robbins is only one of several top professionals who can coach you to excellence, there are a number of competent, effective coaches who can dramatically change your life for the better. Seek them out! Inquire! Ask them for help.

Using excuses as reasons for the lack of success in anything in life is simply a cop-out. I watched a man named Nick Vujicic, who had no feet and no hands, conduct a motivational speaking seminar with incredibly powerful results. Just read his story at www.nickvujicic.com and weep.

If you feel stuck and uninspired, confused about what you should do to get out of the rut you're in, you have to create a paradigm shift in your thinking. Remember, success in life starts with hard work, lots of sweat, fighting through every setback and failure as well as long days and even longer nights of intense focus.

If you are waiting for your ship to come in or some miracle to happen that spontaneously turns your life around, perhaps a stroke of luck like winning the lottery, you have bought into a big lie. Don't do it! Instead, go out and help someone in need, go serve at a soup kitchen, or spend the day with someone homeless and get a taste of how the poor actually live. Take your focus off of yourself and your personal difficulties and reach out to others in desperate circumstances. You'll be surprised how fast your thinking clears and how capable you come to feel as a result of shedding your self-absorption.

I wish I could go into the business offices of the world and take the occupants out for a day in the streets or to a third-world country. The change in them and their perspectives would be immediate. I would love to take the poor and downcast to the homes and offices of the rich and influential to whet their taste buds for the finer things in life. That exposure would be sure to stimulate and motivate them to want to acquire them.

We all have the opportunity to become better people and more successful than we are. We need to develop a passion for life and feel it, sense it, handle it, see it, and then own it. Remember, if you don't like what is growing in your garden, stop planting it. Any excuses you make for not doing something or for why something failed to work as expected, are killing your future successes. Decide that today is a new beginning, and it will be.

Why? Because you have determined it will be, and there is nothing in heaven or hell that is going to stop you.

Always be true to yourself and do what you feel is right. I promise you, you will reap what you sow — good or bad. Sow good seeds every day, plow hard and fast, and always share with others the fruits of your labors.

Always distribute to the poor with your increase, and build some wealth, not just for yourself, but for your children's children.

At bottom, life is so simple. We have made it hard by doubting our own abilities, talents, and toughness. It's a tragic misunderstanding of who we are, why we are here and a waste of what our best intentions can mean to the world. However small and insignificant you may feel, you are here for a reason and have within you God-given assets that, if recognized and used correctly, guarantee your success and your personal contribution to making the world a better place for everyone.

Good Luck to You All

"Keep your face always toward the sunshine—
and shadows will fall behind you."

—Walt Whitman

Chapter 35

Good Luck to You All

That's my story . . . for what it's worth. Thank you for sharing your time with me and reading it. Remember, I wrote this book for you. Revealing so much of my personal life and business record was not easy, and re-visiting so many painful memories was even harder on me. But I was determined to get my story out because I feel it's vital to discuss how destructive, traumatic life experiences, ruinous personal choices, and catastrophic failures can be turned into hard-won life lessons that can serve as a launching pad for your most successful jump.

I know the beginning chapters about my childhood were tough to get through, but I really felt I had to share all the challenges I've had and have eventually overcome, to make my point that you can't let your past control your future or what your life can be.

You can't let your past become an excuse for not being successful and especially for not even trying. If I made it through everything I have in life and could become a good and decent person as well as a successful businessman, I know you can do it too. I am not a victim. I'm a victor!

No matter what you have been through in life or what you are facing right now, do not let it stop you from succeeding in achieving your goals or pursuing your dreams, whatever they are or however ambitious they are. With the right attitude, you and everyone around you will be shocked at what you will accomplish.

Try to gain strength from your challenges. Whatever mistakes you have made, whatever failures or defeats you have experienced, you will learn invaluable lessons from them and acquire real power from having endured them. Don't let your dreams die and, most importantly, never be afraid to jump!

I wish you all the best of luck in your journey and hope in some small way that I may have helped you or inspired you. Now go out there and face life head on.

Jump! Now you will have no excuse.

77412854R00142

Made in the USA
Columbia, SC
21 September 2017